Simply SEVEN COLOURS

ZOLA NENE

Dedicated to my niece, Emily Duduzile van der Westhuizen.

Welcome to the family, little one.

ACKNOWLEDGEMENTS

Thank you to each and every person who bought and cooked from my first two books – I appreciate the love and support more than I could ever properly articulate. Thank you to my awesome publisher for your consistent vote of confidence and for being part of yet another incredible milestone. Thank you, also, for always honouring and respecting my food narrative and vision. A special thank you to my amazing friends, Bas and Matanna, for walking this journey with me again. Thank you for always embracing my book projects like your own and for pouring so much love and joy into them. Cheers to another book on the shelf!

CONTENTS

Zola's feast

FROM THE AUTHOR

Hi, guys! I'm back with a third cookbook... somebody pinch me! *Third* book! This is such a surreal moment; I almost can't believe that I'm back to share even more simple and delicious recipes with you.

It's been a tough couple of years for all of us since the pandemic hit. There is not a single person who hasn't been affected in some way by Covid-19. The resounding lesson I've learnt from it all has definitely been one of gratitude – the pandemic taught me to be grateful for every single moment I have.

Like many others, I've spent most of the last couple of years in a social-distancing bubble with my family. One good thing about the pandemic is how it has brought us so much closer together. I guess times of uncertainty shed light on what is really important, reminding us that time spent with our loved ones is actually what makes life enjoyable. Of course, food is my love language so, for me, spending more quality time with my family meant more cooking and eating... which is why writing this book couldn't have come at a better time.

In *Simply Seven Colours*, I bring you more tasty recipes that tap into our food nostalgia, focusing on going back to basics and celebrating the wonderful tradition of sharing meals. The pandemic drove many people into the kitchen to start cooking again, which I thought was fabulous. It also meant that more people were engaging in conversations about food and exchanging recipes online. In times of difficulty, we look to comfort food, food that hugs us from within, especially when we can't be with the ones nearest and dearest to us. I found that so many more people were looking for and making their moms' or gogos' old recipes, in the spirit of nostalgia for times of togetherness. I loved seeing the shift towards traditional family meals, and the celebration of the colourful, vibrant dishes that define the South African plate.

This book is my tribute to quality time spent sharing meals with loved ones. I hope the recipes will form part of your family food memories for generations to come, and continue to bring you simply delicious joy.

WHAT'S IN A NAME? UKUDLA KWASEKHAYA, SUNDAY LUNCH, SEVEN COLOURS, SEVERAL COLOURS, SONDAG KOS

When I was growing up, Sunday meals were always the most special meal of the week. My family would gather around the dining table to feast on a variety of colourful dishes that my mom spent the morning preparing. We'd chat about the week that was, share jokes, laugh out loud and tell stories, all while enjoying a delicious spread of food. The memories made as we shared those meals is the reason why Sunday meals are still such an important, nostalgic part of my life today.

In my family we referred to this meal as 'Sunday lunch'. Funnily enough, if we had a similar meal during the week, or on any day other than Sunday, we just called it a regular 'lunch' or 'dinner'. There was clearly something extra special about a Sunday meal in my family. It was only later in my life, after learning about other food cultures and how other people experience their family food traditions, that I learnt and adopted the term 'seven colours'. I loved that it described exactly the meals I grew up enjoying with my family, and it sounded much cooler than 'Sunday lunch'! More recently, I learnt through a very heated debate on Twitter that some refer to this meal as 'several colours', the argument being that 'seven' is actually a misnomer of the original 'several'. The truth is, 'several colours' is probably a more apt description of the variety encompassed by the seven-colours meal. This is probably also why one is not actually limited to having only seven colours on the plate, despite the use of the term 'seven colours'; there can be more or less than seven, as long as the meal consists of a variety of colours.

In isiZulu, we call this meal 'ukudla kwasekhaya' but, whichever term you choose to use, the definition is ultimately the same: all refer to a colourful and abundant meal shared with family and friends. So, while we may agree to disagree on the name, we are definitely all on the same page when it comes to the deliciousness that is a colourful plate of food.

In my adult life, I've continued the tradition started by my parents and still make a point of making Sunday lunch a special experience in my home. If you follow my social-media channels (which you should... @zola_nene & @zola_feasts on Instagram and YouTube), you will have seen my #simplyzolasunday posts, which evoke so much excitement in people. I think people resonate with these posts so deeply, because we all grew up enjoying a special meal with our families, whether it was on Sundays, like my family did, monthly, or even just a few times a year on special occasions. The frequency of those meals is less important than the memories made and the positive emotions evoked during the experience of eating and sharing them.

This is why I wanted the theme of my third cookbook to be a celebration of seven colours. I want *Simply Seven Colours* to be your go-to guide to creative and imaginative seven-colour meals.

HAPPY COOKING, AND I WISH YOU MANY SIMPLY DELICIOUS MOMENTS!

HOW TO USE THIS BOOK

The chapters are structured according to different colours. The idea is for you to create your own unique seven-colour menu by picking recipes from different chapters or 'colours'. Each chapter includes a variety of veggies and starches, as well as meat, fish and poultry, making it easy for you to create varying combinations of colourful dishes to feast on at every meal.

ZOLA'S TIPS

- Unless otherwise stipulated, I use olive oil for sautéing and sunflower oil for deep-frying. If a recipe calls simply for 'oil', you can use any oil you like.
- Unless otherwise specified, always sauté over medium heat.
- When sautéing with oil, always add the oil to a hot pot or pan, i.e., heat the pot or pan first before adding the oil, to allow it to warm through before you begin cooking. When cooking with butter, always add the butter to a cold pot or pan and then heat, to prevent the butter from burning.
- Sriracha sauce is my preferred hot sauce. If you can't find sriracha, substitute it with Tabasco® sauce or your favourite hot sauce.
- When a recipe calls simply for 'sugar', you can use granulated white or brown sugar, unless otherwise specified.
- I prefer to use Italian flat-leaf parsley, but you can substitute curly parsley.
- I use vanilla extract, but you can substitute vanilla essence or vanilla paste.

ZOLA'S FEASTS SPICE MIX ALTERNATIVES

I have my own range of spice mixes, which I use throughout this book, and which can be purchased directly from my website (www.zolanene.com). However, unless otherwise specified, you can substitute my Flavourbomb Spice Mix for any Cajun spice blend, or my Fragrant Curry Powder for any mild curry powder.

Fragrant Curry Powder

Flavourbomb Spice Mix

COOKING CONVERSIONS & MEASUREMENTS

IMPERIAL	METRIC
½ tsp	2.5 ml
1 tsp	5 ml
1 Tbsp	15 ml
¼ cup	60 ml
½ cup	125 ml
¾ cup	180 ml
1 cup	250 ml

USEFUL CONVERSIONS

1 cup cake flour = 250 ml = 140 g
1 cup butter = 250 ml = 250 g
1 cup water = 250 ml = 250 g

MEASUREMENTS

Throughout the book, I use the following measurement abbreviations:

- ml = millilitres
- g = grams
- tsp = teaspoon
- Tbsp = tablespoon

MAX&MIA

GREEN

ISIGWAMBA (SPINACH PAP)

SERVES 4

3 Tbsp olive oil
1 onion, chopped
1 garlic clove, crushed
½ tsp dried chilli flakes
1 large bunch (150 g) spinach, rinsed and chopped
Salt and pepper, to taste
1 cup maize meal
3 cups water

1. Heat a pot over medium heat. Add the olive oil and onion, and sauté until soft. Add the garlic and chilli flakes, and sauté until they release their flavour.
2. Toss in the spinach and stir until the leaves are wilted. The leaves will be wet from rinsing, which will create enough steam to cook them sufficiently. Season with salt and pepper to taste.
3. In a bowl, mix the maize meal and water to form a slurry, then stir it into the spinach in the pot. Continue stirring over medium heat until the pap thickens and begins to bubble. Cover with a lid, then lower the heat and simmer for 15–20 minutes, or until cooked through. Season with salt.

ZOLA'S FEASTS SPICED SPINACH & MUSHROOMS

SERVES 4

2 Tbsp olive oil
1 onion, chopped
1 red pepper, pith and seeds removed, and diced
2 Tbsp Zola's Feasts Flavourbomb Spice Mix
½ punnet (125 g) button mushrooms, sliced
1 vegetable stock cube
2 cups chopped frozen spinach
Salt and pepper, to taste

1. Heat a pot over medium heat, then add the olive oil. Add the onion and red pepper, and sauté until the onion softens and begins to brown around the edges. Add the Flavourbomb Spice Mix and mushrooms, and continue to sauté for 5 minutes.
2. Crumble in the stock cube, add the frozen spinach and stir well to combine. Lower the heat, cover with a lid and leave to cook for 5 minutes. Taste for seasoning and add as needed.

CREAMED SPINACH

SERVES 4

1 Tbsp olive oil
30 g butter
1 onion, finely chopped
2 garlic cloves, finely chopped
Pinch dried chilli flakes
1 stock cube (vegetable, chicken or beef)
300 g chopped spinach, fresh or frozen
1 cup fresh cream
Salt and pepper, to taste

1. Heat a pan over medium heat. Add the olive oil, butter and onion, and sauté until softened. Add the garlic and chilli flakes, then crumble in thestock cube.
2. Add the spinach and toss well. Cover the pan with a lid and allow the spinach to wilt for 5 minutes.
3. Stir in the fresh cream, season with salt and pepper, and simmer with the lid off for 15 minutes, to allow the cream to reduce and thicken.

SAUTÉED CABBAGE & SPINACH

SERVES 4

50 g butter
2 Tbsp olive oil
2 Tbsp grated ginger
3 cups shredded cabbage
250 g chopped spinach, fresh or frozen
Salt and pepper, to taste

1. Melt the butter in a pan over medium heat. Add the olive oil and ginger, and sauté for about 10 seconds to release the aroma, before adding the shredded cabbage. Continue sautéing for a few minutes, until the cabbage begins to soften.
2. Add the spinach and sauté until wilted and heated through. Season with salt and pepper.

LEMON & GARLIC SAUTÉED GREEN BEANS

SERVES 4

300 g fresh green beans
3 Tbsp olive oil
1 garlic clove, sliced
4 sprigs fresh thyme
Pinch dried chilli flakes
Zest and juice of 1 lemon
Salt and pepper, to taste

1. Trim the beans then cover with boiling water. Leave to steep for 3 minutes (to blanch the beans and bring out their bright green colour), then drain.
2. Heat a large pan and add the olive oil, garlic, thyme and chilli flakes. Sauté over low heat for 2–3 minutes, to release the flavours of the herbs and spices.
3. Add the drained green beans, increase the heat to high and sauté for 5–6 minutes, or until the beans are cooked through and coated in the aromatic oil. Add the lemon zest and juice, and season with salt and pepper.

CREAMY BRUSSELS SPROUTS

SERVES 4–6

2 Tbsp olive oil
1 onion, sliced
1 tsp cumin seeds
Pinch dried chilli flakes
600 g Brussels sprouts, halved
1 Tbsp sliced garlic
1 cup water
½ cup fresh cream
Salt and pepper, to taste

1. Heat a pan over medium heat. Add the olive oil, onion, garlic, cumin seeds and chilli flakes, and sauté until the onions soften.
2. Add the Brussels sprouts and toss to ensure they are evenly coated in the spices and oil, before adding the water and a pinch of salt. Cover with a lid and simmer for 5 minutes.
3. Stir in the cream, then simmer for 3 minutes, or until the sprouts are cooked through. Season with salt and pepper.

RICE & BABY MARROW FRITTERS

MAKES 8–12

4 cups cooked rice, cooled
2 cups grated baby marrows
125 g cottage cheese
2 spring onions, chopped
2 eggs
30 g fresh herbs (parsley, chives coriander, dill), chopped
Salt and pepper, to taste
Olive oil, for frying

1. In a large bowl, mix together the rice, baby marrows, cottage cheese, spring onions, eggs, fresh herbs, and salt and pepper.
2. Heat a large pan over medium heat and add the olive oil. Dollop spoonfuls of the mixture into the pan and fry until golden on both sides. Don't flip the fritters until they are golden and crisp on the first side (about 3 minutes), or they might break apart.

SPLIT PEA DHAL

SERVES 6–8

400 g green split peas
3 cups cold water
2 Tbsp olive oil
1 onion, chopped
1 garlic clove, chopped
1 Tbsp grated ginger
2 Tbsp garam masala
1 stock cube (vegetable, chicken or beef)
Salt, to taste

1. Rinse the split peas well then add to a pot. Cover with cold water, bring to a boil and simmer for 1 hour (make sure you top up the water as needed – it will slowly evaporate as the split peas cook).
2. Heat a small pot or pan over medium heat. Add the olive oil, onion, garlic and ginger, and sauté until the onions have softened. Add the garam masala and cook for another minute, then add to the pot with the split peas.
3. Add the stock cube, then cover with a lid and simmer gently for 30 minutes. Season with salt.

ORANGE

CUMIN & HONEY-GLAZED CARROTS

SERVES 4–6

500 g carrots
¼ cup water
1 tsp cumin seeds
¼ cup honey
50 g butter
Salt and pepper, to taste

1. Peel the carrots and cut them into chunks. Add the carrots and water to a pan, and cover with a lid. Bring to a boil, then lower the heat and simmer for 20 minutes, or until the carrots are tender.
2. Stir in the cumin seeds, honey and butter. Increase the heat to high and simmer until all the water evaporates, the butter melts and the honey becomes sticky and coats the carrots. Toss continuously during cooking to ensure the carrots are evenly coated.
3. Once the carrots are shiny and glazed, season with salt and pepper.

SWEET POTATO & CORIANDER MASH

SERVES 4

1 kg orange sweet potatoes
Cold water
125 g smooth cottage cheese
4 Tbsp chopped fresh coriander
Salt and pepper, to taste

1. Peel and chop the sweet potatoes, then add them to a large pot and cover with cold water. Bring the water to a boil and cook the sweet potatoes until fork tender (about 20 minutes), then drain in a colander.
2. Return the potatoes to the pot and mash until smooth. Stir in the cottage cheese and coriander, and season with salt and pepper.

CARROT SALAD

SERVES 4

1 red onion, sliced
2 Tbsp white wine vinegar
1 Tbsp white sugar
½ tsp salt
250 g carrots
2 Tbsp chopped coriander

1. In a bowl, combine the onion, white wine vinegar, sugar and salt. Toss well to combine, then set aside to allow the onion to steep for 5 minutes.
2. Peel the carrots, then grate them on the side with the largest grating holes.
3. Add the grated carrots and coriander to the onion mixture and mix until evenly combined.

CINNAMON ROAST PUMPKIN WEDGES

SERVES 4

½ medium (± 1 kg) pumpkin
100 g butter, melted
1 tsp ground cinnamon
¼ tsp ground nutmeg
2 Tbsp honey
¼ cup orange juice (or water)

1. Preheat the oven to 180 °C.
2. Cut the pumpkin into chunky wedges (I leave the skin on, but you can remove it if you prefer). Place the wedges in a single layer on a baking tray or roasting dish.
3. Mix together the melted butter, cinnamon, nutmeg and honey. Brush the pumpkin wedges with the mixture, making sure to coat all sides.
4. Pour over the orange juice, cover the tray with foil, and roast the pumpkin for 30 minutes.
5. After 30 minutes, remove the foil and baste the pumpkin with the juices. Continue to roast, uncovered, for another 30 minutes, or until the pumpkin is soft and lightly browned on top.

ISIJINGI (PUMPKIN PAP)

SERVES 4

1 kg pumpkin, peeled and chopped
Water, enough to cover the pumpkin
1½ cups maize meal
2 cups cold water
1 tsp salt

1. Add the pumpkin to a large pot, cover with water and bring to a boil. Once cooked, use a colander to drain the pumpkin of excess water. Return the pumpkin to the pot and mash.
2. Mix the maize meal with the cold water to make a slurry. Add the mixture and salt to the mashed pumpkin.
3. Place the pot over medium heat and cook, stirring continuously, until it comes to a simmer. Cover with a lid, then lower the heat and continue to simmer for 45 minutes, stirring occasionally.

CHICKPEA-STUFFED BUTTERNUT

SERVES 4 AS A MAIN AND 8 AS A SIDE

2 medium (± 2 kg) butternuts
2 Tbsp olive oil
Salt and pepper, to taste
1 cup water
1 can (410 g) chickpeas, drained and rinsed
3 spring onions, chopped
1 cup grated cheddar cheese, plus extra for sprinkling

1. Preheat the oven to 180 °C.
2. Cut the butternuts in half lengthways, remove the seeds, then score the flesh with a sharp knife. Drizzle each half with olive oil, and season with salt and pepper.
3. Place the halved butternuts on a baking tray. Pour the water into the tray, cover with foil, then bake in the oven for 1½ hours, or until soft.
4. Once fully cooked, remove the butternuts from the oven. Carefully scoop the butternut flesh out of its skin. Make sure you keep the skins intact, which you can do by leaving a 5 mm border of flesh around the inside of the skin. Set the skins aside for later.
5. Mix the butternut flesh with the chickpeas, spring onions and cheddar cheese until well combined. Season to taste.
6. Spoon the butternut and chickpea mixture back into the butternut skins, sprinkle with more cheddar cheese, and return to the baking tray (or roasting dish). Bake for a further 30 minutes, until the cheese has melted and browned on top.

APRICOT & ORANGE-GLAZED SNOEK

SERVES 4–6

¼ cup apricot jam
Juice of 1 orange
Juice of ½ lemon
1 Tbsp grated ginger
1 garlic clove, minced
1 Tbsp butter
2 Tbsp chopped fresh parsley
1 snoek (± 700 g), butterflied

1. In a saucepan, combine the apricot jam, orange juice, lemon juice, ginger, garlic and butter. Simmer over medium heat until the butter is melted. Stir in the chopped parsley. Set aside half of the glaze to serve with the snoek.
2. Brush some of the remaining glaze onto the flesh of the snoek, then place it on a hinged braai grid. With the snoek flesh-side down, place the grid over medium coals for 6 minutes. Carefully turn over, then brush with more of the glaze while cooking for another 6 minutes. Alternatively, roast the snoek in the oven at 200 °C for 20 minutes, basting with the glaze halfway through. Serve the remaining glaze on the side.

CHICKEN & APRICOT SOSATIES

SERVES 4–6

6 wooden sosatie sticks
1 Tbsp Zola's Feasts Flavourbomb Spice Mix
½ cup fruit chutney
Fresh chilli, chopped, to taste
Salt and pepper, to taste
4 chicken breast fillets, cut into chunks
18 Turkish (soft-dried) dried apricots

1. Soak the sosatie sticks in water for 10 minutes. This will prevent them from burning when you cook the chicken.
2. Mix together the Flavourbomb Spice Mix, chutney, fresh chilli, and salt and pepper. Add the chunks of chicken and mix into the marinade until evenly coated.
3. Skewer the chicken onto the sosatie sticks, alternating with the apricots. You can leave the sosaties to marinate overnight at this stage, if you wish.
4. Cook the sosaties on the braai over medium coals or in a griddle pan until the chicken is cooked through and golden.

SPICY PRAWNS
WITH LEMON & GARLIC-MAYO DIP

SERVES 4

FOR THE PRAWNS

¼ cup sweet chilli sauce
3 Tbsp olive oil
Juice of 1 lemon
2 Tbsp smoked paprika
2 tsp lemon pepper
1 tsp cayenne pepper
Salt, to taste
500 g large prawns, deveined

FOR THE GARLIC-MAYO DIP

½ cup mayonnaise
½ cup sour cream
Zest and juice of 1 lemon
2 Tbsp chopped fresh parsley
1 tsp chopped garlic
Salt and pepper, to taste

1. To make the prawns, combine the sweet chilli sauce, olive oil, lemon juice, paprika, lemon pepper, cayenne pepper and salt in a bowl. Add the prawns and toss well to coat (remove the shells first, if you prefer).
2. Heat a griddle pan over high heat. Grill the prawns until cooked through and charred on both sides.
3. To make the mayo dip, mix all the ingredients until well combined. Serve the prawns hot with the dip.

MARMALADE-GLAZED GAMMON

SERVES 4–6

1 orange
2 kg boneless uncooked gammon
4 slices ginger
2 bay leaves
4 cloves
Water, enough to cover the gammon
1 Tbsp chopped ginger
¼ cup sugar
½ cup orange marmalade
Salt and pepper, to taste

1. Grate the zest of the orange and set aside. Cut the orange in half. Juice one half and set the juice aside. Slice the remaining half of the orange.
2. Place the gammon, orange zest, orange slices, sliced ginger, bay leaves and cloves in a large pot, then cover with water. Place a lid on the pot and bring to a boil over hight heat, then reduce the heat to medium and simmer for 1 hour. Remove the gammon from the pot, discard the rest, then remove the netting/string from the gammon.
3. Preheat the oven to 200 °C.
4. Cut the skin off the gammon. Remove any excess fat and discard. Mix together the orange juice, chopped ginger, sugar and marmalade, and season with salt and pepper.
5. Place the gammon in a roasting dish. Brush the glaze over the gammon, then roast in the oven for 30–40 minutes. Baste halfway through, after 15–20 minutes, then continue roasting until the glaze becomes sticky and golden. Once cooked, baste the gammon for a final time, allow to rest for 10 minutes, then carve and serve.

YELLOW

BUTTERY GEM SQUASH MASH

SERVES 4

6 gem squash
½ cup water
60 g butter,
  plus extra to serve
½ cup fresh cream
Salt, to taste

1. Cut the gem squash in half and place them, cut-side down, in a microwave-safe bowl. Add the water and cover with cling wrap. Cook the squash in the microwave on high power for 12–15 minutes. Test if they are cooked by piercing the flesh with a fork – it should be tender. Remove from the microwave and allow to cool for a few minutes.
2. Scoop the seeds out of the gem squash and discard.
3. Add the butter, cream and a pinch of salt to a saucepan, then bring to a simmer. Scoop the flesh of the gem squash into the warmed cream mixture, and mash with a fork until smooth and combined. Serve with an extra knob of butter on top.

CREAMY SAMP

SERVES 4

2 cups dried samp
2 cups boiling water
2 bay leaves
Pinch saffron
  (or ½ tsp turmeric)
Cold water
¼ cup fresh cream
Salt, to taste

1. Place the samp in a bowl, cover with boiling water and soak for 30 minutes. (Or soak in cold water for 24 hours.)
2. Rinse the soaked samp and add it to a pot. Add the bay leaves, saffron (or turmeric) and cover with cold water. Bring to a boil, then lower the heat and simmer for 1 hour, checking halfway through to top up the water if necessary.
3. After 1 hour, stir the samp – the kernels will be softer, but not quite cooked through, and the starch will have released from the samp and thickened the mixture. Add more water to cover, then simmer for another 30 minutes.
4. Check if the samp is cooked, either by tasting a few kernels (they should be tender) or by mashing some with a fork (they should mash easily).
5. Stir in the fresh cream and season generously with salt. Simmer for 5 minutes before serving.

BUTTERY GEM
SQUASH MASH
CREAMY SAMP

BROWN BUTTER CAULIFLOWER CHEESE

SERVES 4

100 g butter
¼ cup flour
3 cups milk
Salt and pepper, to taste
1 head (± 450 g) cauliflower, cut into florets
200 g grated cheese
(100 g mature cheddar + 100 g mozzarella)

1. Preheat the oven to 200 °C.
2. Melt the butter in a saucepan over medium heat. Once it has melted, increase the heat and allow the butter to bubble and sizzle until it turns a nutty brown colour. Remove from the heat.
3. Stir in the flour until well incorporated. Whisk in the milk, then simmer over medium heat for 8 minutes to cook the sauce. Season with salt and pepper.
4. Stir in the cauliflower florets and grated cheese (reserve some to sprinkle on top). Transfer to an ovenproof dish and sprinkle with the remaining cheese. Cover with foil or a lid and bake for 25 minutes.
5. Remove the cover then bake for another 10 minutes, until the cheese on top is melted and golden.

CHEESY STUFFED POTATOES

SERVES 4

4 medium potatoes
Salt and pepper, to taste
1 cup sour cream
150 g mature cheddar cheese, grated
2 spring onions, chopped, plus extra to garnish
Fresh chilli, chopped, to taste (optional)

1. Wash the potatoes, then prick each one multiple times with a fork. Place them in the microwave, directly onto the plate, then cook on high for 8–10 minutes, or until the potatoes are soft and cooked through.
2. Preheat the oven to 200 °C.
3. Cut the potatoes in half. Carefully scoop out the flesh and place it into a bowl, leaving a thin (± 1–2 mm) border around the skins so they remain intact (the skins will become the carrier for the filling). Place the skins onto a baking tray.
4. In the bowl, lightly mash the potato flesh. Mix in the sour cream, cheddar cheese (reserve some for sprinkling on top), spring onions, and season with salt and pepper. Add the chilli, if using.
5. Spoon the mash into the potato skins, sprinkle with the remaining cheese, and bake for 20–25 minutes, until the cheese is melted and golden. Garnish with spring onion.

SPICED RICE

SERVES 4–6

- 1 cup rice
- 2 cups boiling water
- 2 Tbsp olive oil
- 1 onion, chopped
- 1 red pepper, pith removed, and chopped
- 2 garlic cloves, chopped
- 1½ Tbsp Zola's Feasts Flavourbomb Spice Mix (or spice for rice)
- ½ tsp turmeric
- 1 vegetable stock cube, dissolved in 2 cups hot water

1. Place the rice into a bowl, cover with boiling water and set aside.
2. Heat a pot over medium heat. Add the olive oil, onion and red pepper, and sauté until softened. Add the garlic, Flavourbomb Spice Mix and turmeric, and continue to sauté for another minute.
3. Drain and rinse the soaked rice. Add it to the pot and stir until evenly coated in the spices.
4. Add the vegetable stock, stir well, then cover with a lid and bring to a simmer. Lower the heat and cook for 15–20 minutes, or until the stock is fully absorbed and the rice is cooked through.
5. Turn off the heat, then leave the rice to steam with the lid on for 10 minutes. Fluff the rice with a fork before serving.

FRIED RICE

SERVES 4

2 Tbsp canola oil
3 eggs, beaten
1 onion, sliced
1 carrot, diced
1 Tbsp crushed garlic
1 Tbsp ginger, grated
3 cups cooked rice, cooled
1 Tbsp soy sauce
2 Tbsp sweet chilli sauce
1 tsp sesame oil
3 spring onions, sliced
100 g cherry tomatoes, quartered
2 Tbsp sesame seeds, toasted

1. Heat a pan and add 1 tablespoon of oil. Add the eggs, stirring to scramble until set. Remove from the pan and set aside.
2. To the same pan, add the remaining oil. Add the onion and carrot, and stir-fry until softened. Stir in the garlic, ginger and rice, and stir-fry until the rice is heated through.
3. Stir in the soy sauce, sweet chilli sauce, sesame oil, spring onions and cherry tomatoes. Fold in the scrambled egg. Sprinkle with toasted sesame seeds and serve.

MICROWAVE SWEETCORN & CHEDDAR RISOTTO

SERVES 4

2 Tbsp olive oil
20 g butter
1 onion, finely chopped
2 garlic cloves, crushed
2 tsp chopped fresh thyme
1½ cups arborio or risotto rice
4 cups vegetable stock
1 can (410 g) creamed sweetcorn
100 g mature cheddar cheese, grated
Salt and pepper, to taste

1. Place the olive oil, butter, onion, garlic and thyme into a large microwave-safe dish, then microwave on high for 4 minutes. The onion should be softened and translucent (if not, cook for 1–2 minutes more).
2. Stir in the rice and vegetable stock. Return to the microwave and cook for 6 minutes on high.
3. Stir in the creamed sweetcorn and return to the microwave to cook for 12 minutes on high, stirring after 6 minutes. Stir in the cheddar cheese.
4. Remove the dish from the microwave, cover and leave to rest for 2 minutes. Stir, season with salt and pepper, and serve.

CHORIZO MAC & CHEESE

SERVES 4–6

250 g chorizo sausage
1 Tbsp olive oil
80 g butter
¼ cup flour
3 cups milk
200 g cheddar cheese, grated
Salt and pepper, to taste
500 g macaroni or penne pasta
1 punnet (250 g) cherry tomatoes, sliced
Handful fresh basil, chopped

1. Preheat the oven to 180 °C.
2. Chop the chorizo into pieces and add them to a pan, along with the olive oil. Fry over medium heat for 3–4 minutes, or until crisp around the edges. Set aside.
3. Melt the butter in a saucepan, then stir in the flour and cook for 1 minute. Whisk in the milk, stirring continuously until the sauce thickens and bubbles. Simmer for 5 minutes, then stir in about three quarters of the grated cheddar cheese, and season with salt and pepper.
4. Cook the pasta in boiling, salted water for 6 minutes, then drain – don't overcook the pasta at this stage, as it will continue to cook in the oven.
5. Stir the cooked pasta and fried chorizo into the sauce. Transfer to an ovenproof dish and sprinkle with the remaining cheese.
6. In a bowl, mix together the sliced cherry tomatoes and basil, and season with salt and pepper. Scatter this over the pasta.
7. Bake in the oven for 20–30 minutes until bubbling, and the cheese is melted and golden-brown.

GRILLED CORN & CHEESE PAP

SERVES 4–6

- 1½ cups maize meal
- 3 cups water
- 1 tsp salt
- 1 cup frozen corn kernels
- 1 cup grated cheddar cheese
- 2 Tbsp olive oil, for greasing and cooking

1. Add the maize meal and 1 cup of water to a bowl. Stir until well combined.
2. Add the remaining water and salt to a pot, and bring to a boil. Once the water is boiling, add the maize meal slurry and stir well until the mixture thickens. Cover with a lid, lower the heat, and cook for 30 minutes, stirring every 10 minutes.
3. Stir in the corn and cheddar cheese, and mix well to combine. Transfer the mixture to an oiled dish, press down to flatten, and leave to cool to room temperature.
4. Once cooled, cut the pap into thick slices, then brush with olive oil before cooking on a hot griddle pan or on the braai, until charred.

CHEESY RICE-STUFFED MUSHROOMS

SERVES 4

4 large brown mushrooms
Salt and pepper, to taste
2 Tbsp olive oil, plus 1 tsp for greasing
2 cups cooked rice
100 g cheddar cheese, grated
125 g plain cream cheese
2 tsp chopped garlic
3 Tbsp chopped fresh coriander
1 Tbsp chopped fresh thyme

1. Preheat the oven to 180 °C.
2. Place the mushrooms, gill-side up, on a greased oven tray. Season the mushrooms with salt and pepper, then drizzle with olive oil and roast for 20 minutes, until the mushrooms are tender.
3. In a bowl, mix together the cooked rice, cheddar cheese (reserve some for sprinkling on top later), cream cheese, garlic, coriander and thyme. Season with salt and pepper.
4. Spoon the mixture onto the mushrooms and sprinkle with the remaining cheddar cheese.
5. Bake the stuffed mushrooms for 30 minutes, until the cheese on top is golden and bubbling.

SPINACH & MUSHROOM PHYLLO TART

SERVES 6–8

¼ cup olive oil, plus 2 Tbsp
2 sprigs fresh rosemary
1 garlic clove, chopped
250 g mushrooms, sliced
2 Tbsp Zola's Feasts Flavourbomb Spice Mix
400 g spinach, rinsed and chopped
250 g cream cheese, room temperature
½ cup grated cheddar cheese
Salt and pepper, to taste
2 large eggs
4 sheets phyllo pastry

1. Preheat the oven to 180 °C.
2. Add ¼ cup of olive oil, the rosemary and garlic to a saucepan. Heat gently over low heat until the garlic begins to sizzle, then turn off the heat and set aside to infuse.
3. Heat a large pan, then add the remaining 2 tablespoons of olive oil. Add the mushrooms and sauté on high heat until they begin to brown around the edges. Add the Flavourbomb Spice Mix and sauté for a few seconds more to release the aroma of the spices.
4. Add the spinach to the pan and toss well until wilted, and any water from the leaves evaporates.
5. In a bowl, mix together the cream cheese and cheddar cheese, then season with salt and pepper. Mix in the eggs.
6. To the cheese and egg mixture, add the spinach and mushroom mixture, and stir well to combine.
7. Brush each sheet of phyllo pastry with the garlic-and-rosemary infused olive oil, then stack them in a crisscross pattern.
8. Grease a 20 cm loose-bottom, round cake tin with the garlic-and-rosemary infused olive oil, then line with the stack of phyllo pastry sheets. Add the filling, pressing down to avoid air pockets.
9. Place the cake tin on a baking tray and bake in the oven for 30 minutes, until the pastry is golden and the filling is set with no jiggle. Leave to cool to room temperature before slicing and serving.

ONE-POT CHICKEN & RICE

SERVES 4

8 skinless chicken thighs, bone-in
2 Tbsp ground coriander
1 Tbsp ground cumin
1 tsp paprika
Salt and pepper, to taste
2 Tbsp olive oil
1 onion, sliced
2 garlic cloves, sliced
1 Tbsp grated ginger
Pinch dried chilli flakes
1 tsp turmeric
2 tomatoes, grated
1½ cups uncooked basmati rice, rinsed
¼ cup seedless raisins
2 cups chicken stock
3 Tbsp chopped fresh coriander
2 Tbsp toasted flaked almonds

1. Season the chicken thighs with the coriander, cumin, paprika, and salt and pepper. Toss well to coat the chicken in the spices.
2. Heat a pot over medium heat and add the olive oil. Add the chicken thighs and brown for a few minutes on each side. (The chicken doesn't need to be fully cooked at this stage, just browned.) Remove from the pot and set aside.
3. To the same pot, add the onion, garlic, ginger and chilli flakes. Sauté over low heat until the onions begin to soften. Increase the heat to medium, then add the turmeric and tomatoes, and sauté for a few minutes.
4. Stir in the rice, raisins and chicken stock. Return the chicken thighs to the pot, cover with a lid and simmer over medium heat for 15–20 minutes, or until the rice has absorbed all the liquid and the chicken is cooked through.
5. Season with salt and pepper, and sprinkle with fresh chopped coriander and toasted flaked almond before serving.

PICKLED FISH

SERVES 4–6

½ cup cake flour
Salt and pepper, to taste
500 g fish fillets (I used hake)
3 Tbsp vegetable oil
2 onions, sliced
3 bay leaves
1 tsp whole black peppercorns
3 Tbsp Zola's Feasts Fragrant Curry Powder
1 tsp turmeric
¾ cup white sugar
1 cup white spirit vinegar

1. Season the flour with salt and pepper. Coat the fish fillets in the seasoned flour.
2. Heat a pot over medium heat and add the oil. Add the fish fillets and fry until golden on both sides. (The fish doesn't need to be fully cooked at this stage.) Remove from the pan and set aside.
3. To the same pot, add more oil if needed, then add the onions, bay leaves and peppercorns. Sauté for a few minutes, until the onions begin to soften.
4. Add the Fragrant Curry Powder and turmeric, and sauté for a few minutes more to release the aroma of the spices. Add the sugar and white spirit vinegar and bring to a simmer.
5. Return the fish fillets to the pot, cover with a lid and simmer for 5 minutes, until the fish is cooked through.
6. Turn off the heat and leave the pickled fish to cool to room temperature before transferring to the fridge. Refrigerate overnight before serving. The longer the pickled fish is left to sit, the more the flavour will develop. This dish will keep in the fridge for up to 1 week.

CHILLI
WITH AVO-CORNBREAD TOPPING

SERVES 6–8

FOR THE CHILLI
2 Tbsp olive oil
1 onion, chopped
½ red pepper, pith removed, and diced
½ yellow pepper, pith removed, and diced
2 garlic cloves, chopped
500 g mince (I used beef, but you can use chicken or ostrich mince)
1 Tbsp ground cumin
1 Tbsp ground coriander
1 Tbsp paprika
½ tsp dried chilli flakes
1 can (410 g) kidney beans, drained
300 ml beef stock
Salt and pepper, to taste

FOR THE CORNBREAD
1 avocado, mashed
1 cup creamed sweetcorn
1 large egg
¼ cup vegetable or sunflower oil
1 cup amasi or buttermilk
1 Tbsp sugar
2 cups cake flour
2 tsp baking powder
Pinch salt

TO SERVE
Avocado, sliced
Sour cream

1. To make the chilli, sauté the onion, red and yellow peppers, and garlic in the olive oil over medium heat until softened. Add the mince and sauté until browned.
2. Stir in the cumin, coriander, paprika and chilli flakes.
3. Add the kidney beans and stock, then simmer for 15–20 minutes. Season to taste. Transfer the chilli to an ovenproof dish and set aside.
4. Preheat the oven to 180 °C.
5. To make the cornbread topping, combine the mashed avocado, creamed sweetcorn, egg, oil, amasi and sugar in a bowl, and mix until well combined.
6. Add the cake flour, baking powder and salt, and mix until just combined.
7. Spoon the cornbread batter over the chilli and spread evenly to cover. Bake in the oven for 45–50 minutes, or until the cornbread is golden and cooked through. Serve with extra sliced avocado and a dollop of sour cream.

ISINKWA SOMMBILA (STEAMED MEALIE BREAD)

MAKES 1 LOAF

Butter, for greasing
4 mealie cobs (use either fresh white mealies or fresh yellow corn)
2 large eggs
300 ml milk
1 tsp salt
2 tsp white sugar
500 g cake flour
2 tsp baking powder

1. Grease a round cake tin (± 10 cm) with butter. Cut the kernels off the mealie cobs. Grind half the kernels in a food processor or with a pestle and mortar into a coarse paste.
2. In a bowl, combine the ground and whole mealie kernels, eggs and milk.
3. In another bowl, sift together the salt, sugar, flour and baking powder. Add this to the mealie mixture. Stir to combine, but make sure to not overmix.
4. Spoon the mixture into the prepared loaf pan, then place the pan into a large pot of boiling water that reaches halfway up the side of the pan. Cover the pot with a lid and simmer for 1½ hours, topping up the water during cooking if needed.

GARLIC BREAD

SERVES 4

1 French loaf
250 g butter, softened + 50 g, melted
125 g cream cheese, room temperature
4 garlic cloves, minced
Handful fresh parsley, chopped

1. Preheat the oven to 180 °C.
2. Slice the French loaf, making sure not to cut all the way through.
3. Mix together the softened butter, cream cheese, garlic and parsley. Generously spread the mixture between the slices of bread.
4. Brush the top of the loaf with melted butter and wrap in foil. Bake in the oven for 20–25 minutes, until the buttery filling is oozy and warm.

WHITE

GARLIC BUTTER NAAN

MAKES 8

FOR THE NAAN

3 cups cake flour
10 g instant dry yeast
2 tsp sugar
1 tsp salt
⅓ cup plain yoghurt
⅓ cup canola oil, plus extra for greasing
1 egg
± 1½ cups lukewarm water

FOR THE GARLIC BUTTER

300 g butter
6 garlic cloves, chopped

1. To make the naan, whisk together the cake flour, yeast, sugar and salt in a bowl.
2. In a separate bowl, mix together the yoghurt, oil and egg. Add to the dry ingredients and mix well.
3. Slowly add enough lukewarm water to form a soft dough. Knead the dough for about 10 minutes, until it is smooth and elastic. Place the dough into a greased bowl, cover with a damp cloth or cling wrap and leave to prove until the dough has doubled in size.
4. To make the garlic butter, add the butter and chopped garlic to a saucepan. Cook over low heat until the butter has melted, then simmer gently for 5 minutes.
5. Divide the dough into 8 equal pieces, form into balls, then roll out into circles.
6. Heat a heavy-bottomed pan over medium heat. Cook the naan, one at a time, for about 6 minutes on each side, until puffed and browned. Once cooked, remove from the pan and brush with garlic butter on both sides. Wrap each naan in foil to keep warm while you cook the rest.

ROTI

MAKES 12

4 cups cake flour
1½ Tbsp salt
2 Tbsp canola oil
± 2 cups boiling water
100 g butter, melted and slightly cooled

1. In a bowl, mix together the flour and salt. Add the oil and 1 cup of boiling water, and mix. While mixing, add more water, a little at a time, until a soft dough forms (add more water if the dough is too dry).
2. Turn out the dough onto a lightly floured surface and knead for 5 minutes, until it is smooth and elastic. Dust the dough with more flour, then roll it out into a large rectangle.
3. Brush the dough with the butter, then roll it into a log, encasing the butter as you do so. Pinch the seam to seal the log, then refrigerate for 30 minutes to allow the butter to set.
4. Once chilled, cut the log into 12 even slices. Use your hands to stretch out each slice, then tie into a knot.
5. On a floured surface, use a rolling pin to roll out each knotted piece of dough to form a thin circle.
6. Heat a heavy-bottomed pan on high heat. Cook the rotis one at a time for about 3 minutes on the first side, until puffed and blistered, before turning to cook on the other side for another 3 minutes, until cooked through.

UJEQE (STEAMED BREAD)

4 cups cake flour
10 g instant dry yeast
1 Tbsp white sugar
1 tsp salt
± 2½ cups warm water
Butter, softened, for greasing

1. In a bowl, whisk together the cake flour, yeast, sugar and salt. Slowly add the warm water, a little at a time, until a soft dough forms (you might need more or less water).
2. Turn out the dough onto a floured surface and knead for about 10 minutes, until it is smooth and elastic.
3. Place the dough into a bowl greased with butter. Cover with cling wrap and allow to prove for 30 minutes, or until the dough doubles in size.
4. Turn out the dough again onto the floured surface and knead to knock out the air, then form it into a ball. Place it in a heatproof bowl, cover with cling wrap, then leave again to rise until it doubles in size.
5. Place the heatproof bowl into a pot filled with enough boiling water to reach halfway up the bowl. Cover with a lid and simmer for 1½–2 hours, or until a skewer inserted into the centre of the jeqe comes out clean and the bread springs back to the touch. Top up the water in the pot while cooking, if necessary.

AROMATIC RICE

SERVES 4

1 cup long-grain rice, rinsed
4 cups water
1 tsp salt
100 g butter
3 cardamom pods, cracked
1 cinnamon stick, broken in half
2 tsp aniseed
Salt, to taste

1. Add the rice, water and salt to a pot. Bring to a boil, then cook for about 20 minutes, or until the rice is tender. Once cooked, drain the rice in a colander.
2. To a large pan, add the butter, cardamom, cinnamon and aniseed. Turn on the heat and stir as the butter melts. As soon as the butter begins to brown, turn off the heat and toss in the rice. Use a fork to stir and fluff the rice with the spices. Season with salt to taste.

IKABISHI
UPHUTHU

UPHUTHU
(CRUMBLY MEALIE MEAL)

SERVES 4

2 cups water
1 tsp salt
4 cups maize meal

1. Add the water and salt to a large pot and bring to a boil. While the water is boiling, pour in all of the maize meal at once, then stir well to mix (I use the handle of a wooden spoon). There should be no dry mealie meal left and the mealie meal will form into clumps.
2. Reduce the heat to the lowest setting. Cover the pot with a lid and cook for about 30 minutes, stirring every 10 minutes to ensure it cooks evenly. The mealie meal will smell nutty and a thin crust will form on the bottom of the pot when it is ready to serve – this is meant to happen, but it should not be burnt.

IKABISHI NAMAZAMBANE
(CABBAGE & POTATOES)

SERVES 4

2 Tbsp oil
1 onion, sliced
1 tsp chopped garlic
1 Tbsp Zola's Feasts Fragrant Curry Powder
2 potatoes, peeled and chopped
1 vegetable stock cube, dissolved in 1½ cups hot water
½ head white cabbage, chopped

1. Heat a pan over medium heat. Add the oil and onion, and fry until soft. Add the garlic and curry powder, and sauté for 1 minute. Add the potatoes and stir to coat them evenly in the spices.
2. Stir in the vegetable stock, cover with a lid and simmer for 5 minutes.
3. Add the chopped cabbage, stir, then cover again and cook for another 10 minutes, until the cabbage is tender and the potatoes are cooked through.

MUSHROOM & GARLIC SAMP

SERVES 4

2 cups dried samp
4 cups water
¼ cup extra-virgin olive oil
1 onion, sliced
½ punnet (125 g) button mushrooms, sliced
2 garlic cloves, chopped
1 Tbsp dried origanum
1 cup vegetable or chicken stock
Salt and pepper, to taste

1. Wash the samp, then add it to a pot and cover with the water. Bring to a boil, then simmer over medium heat for about 1½ hours, or until the samp is tender. (You might need to top up the water during cooking.) Drain the cooked samp and set aside.
2. Heat a large pan over medium heat and add the olive oil, onion and mushrooms. Sauté until they have softened and begun to brown around the edges. Add the garlic and origanum, and sauté for another minute.
3. Add the cooked samp and stock, cover with a lid and simmer for 10 minutes.
4. Season the cooked samp with salt and pepper before serving.

CAULIFLOWER STEAKS
WITH MUSTARD CREAM & TOASTED ALMONDS

SERVES 4

1 head cauliflower,
cut into thick steaks
1 Tbsp olive oil
1 Tbsp butter
Salt and pepper, to taste
Pinch dried chilli flakes
1 tsp cumin seeds
1 cup sour cream
2 Tbsp wholegrain mustard
1 Tbsp honey
50 g toasted almond flakes

1. Preheat the oven to 180 °C.
2. To make the cauliflower steaks, heat a pan over medium heat, then add the olive oil and butter. Place the cauliflower steaks in the pan and brown on each side for 2 minutes until golden. Season with salt and pepper and chilli flakes, and sprinkle with cumin seeds. Transfer the steaks to an ovenproof dish and roast in the oven for 20 minutes.
3. To make the mustard cream, mix together the sour cream, wholegrain mustard and honey, and season with salt and pepper.
4. To serve, spread a generous amount of the mustard cream onto a plate, top with a cauliflower steak, and finish with a sprinkle of toasted almond flakes.

BROWN

UBHONTSHISI (CURRIED BEAN STEW)

SERVES 4–6

2 cups dried sugar beans, washed
Cold water
2 Tbsp olive oil
300 g beef short rib, bone-in (optional)
1 onion, chopped
2 bay leaves
2 garlic cloves, chopped
1 Tbsp grated ginger
4 sprigs fresh thyme
2 Tbsp Zola's Feasts Fragrant Curry Powder
1 stock cube (beef or vegetable)
Salt and pepper, to taste

1. Add the sugar beans to a pot, cover with cold water and bring to a boil. Leave the beans to boil for 1½ hours. (You might need to top up the water to make sure it doesn't boil away.)
2. Heat another pot over medium heat. Add the olive oil and short rib (if using) and fry for 15–20 minutes, until browned all over.
3. Add the onion and sauté until soft. Stir in the bay leaves, garlic, ginger, thyme and curry powder, and cook over low heat for 1–2 minutes, to release the flavour of the spices (do not burn).
4. Add the cooked beans, stock cube and more water to cover the beans. Simmer for another hour, until the beans and meat (if using) are tender. Season with salt and pepper.

FISH CURRY

SERVES 4

2 Tbsp sunflower or coconut oil
1 onion, sliced
1 Tbsp chopped garlic
1 Tbsp chopped ginger
1 Tbsp ground cumin
2 Tbsp ground coriander
1 Tbsp chilli powder (or to taste)
1 can (400 g) chopped tomatoes
1 Tbsp sugar
1 can (400 ml) coconut milk
Salt and pepper, to taste
500 g fish fillets (I used hake, but any firm white fish will do)
Juice of ½ lime
20 g fresh coriander, chopped, plus extra, to garnish

1. Heat a pot over medium heat and add the oil. Add the onion and sauté until soft and brown around the edges, then add the garlic, ginger, cumin, coriander and chilli powder, and sauté for another minute.
2. Stir in the tomatoes and sugar, and simmer for 5 minutes.
3. Stir in the coconut milk, season with salt and pepper, and simmer for another 5 minutes.
4. Gently stir in the fish fillets and poach for 4–5 minutes, until the fish is cooked through. Stir in the lime juice and coriander just before serving.

PILCHARD FISH CAKES

MAKES 4

3 potatoes, boiled and mashed (yields 1½ cups mash)
2 spring onions, chopped
20 g fresh coriander, chopped
1 garlic clove, chopped (optional)
1 can (400 g) pilchards in tomato sauce (reserve the sauce)
1 egg, beaten
Salt and pepper, to taste
¼ cup oil
Lemon wedges, to serve

1. Mix together the mashed potatoes, spring onions, coriander, garlic, pilchards, egg, and salt and pepper. Form the mixture into patties, then refrigerate for 30 minutes to set.
2. Heat a pan and add the oil. Fry the fish cakes for 5 minutes on each side, until golden and crispy. Serve with the reserved sauce (heat it first) and lemon wedges.

COCONUT CURRY MUSSELS

SERVES 4

2 Tbsp olive oil
1 onion, finely chopped
1 Tbsp grated ginger
1 Tbsp chopped garlic
1 chilli, halved
2 Tbsp Zola's Feasts Fragrant Curry Powder
1 can (400 ml) coconut milk
Salt and pepper, to taste
1 kg whole fresh or frozen mussels
1 lemon
20 g fresh coriander, chopped

1. Heat a pot over medium heat. Add the olive oil, onion, ginger, garlic and chilli, and sauté until softened.
2. Add the Fragrant Curry Powder, lower the heat and sauté for 1 minute to release the aroma of the spices.
3. Stir in the coconut milk, season with salt and pepper, then bring to a simmer. Stir in the mussels and add a squeeze of lemon juice. Cover the pot with a lid and leave to simmer until the mussels have opened and are cooked through.
4. Stir in the coriander and a final squeeze of lemon juice, and serve.

CRISPY FRIED CHICKEN WINGS

SERVES 4

16 chicken wings
2 cups amasi (or buttermilk)
¼ cup sriracha sauce
8 Tbsp Zola's Feasts Flavourbomb Spice Mix
3 cups flour
Salt and pepper, to taste
4 cups oil

1. Place the chicken wings in a bowl, then add the amasi (or buttermilk), sriracha and 4 tablespoons of the Flavourbomb Spice Mix. Leave the chicken to marinate for at least 2 hours, or preferably overnight.
2. Mix together the flour, remaining Flavourbomb Spice Mix, and salt and pepper. Stir 2 tablespoons of the marinade into the flour mixture until large flakes form.
3. Dip each chicken wing into the flour flakes, making sure each one is coated well.
4. Heat the oil in a pot and deep-fry the wings until golden brown and cooked through. Make sure the oil isn't too hot or the outside will burn before the inside cooks – about 180 °C is the ideal oil temperature for frying. If you don't have a cooking thermometer, place a wooden spoon into the oil. If the oil bubbles around the spoon, it is hot enough. Drain the wings on paper towel before serving.

CHUTNEY CHICKEN

SERVES 4

8 chicken pieces, bone-in and skin-on
1 Tbsp olive oil
2 Tbsp Zola's Feasts Flavourbomb Spice Mix
1 cup fruit chutney
Juice of ½ lemon
½ cup water

1. Drizzle the chicken with olive oil. Sprinkle each piece with the Flavourbomb Spice Mix and toss well to coat.
2. Heat a pan, then add the chicken and brown on all sides until golden.
3. Whisk together the chutney, lemon juice and water, then pour the mixture over the chicken.
4. Cover the pan with a lid and simmer gently over medium heat for 15 minutes. Remove the lid, turn up the heat and continue to simmer with the lid off until the sauce becomes thick and sticky. Turn the chicken as the sauce reduces and thickens so it coats the chicken evenly.

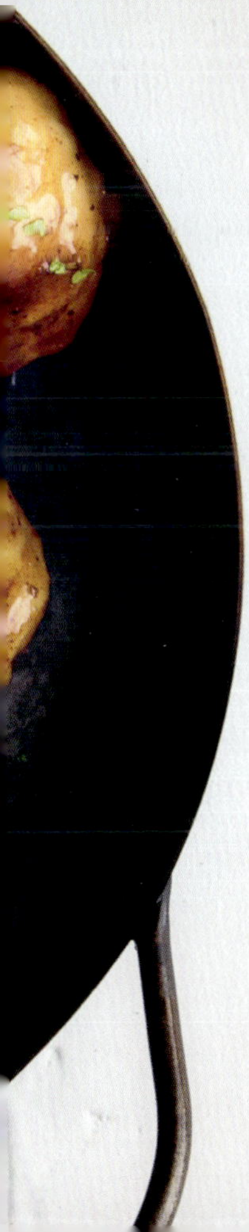

YOGHURT & HERB MARINATED CHICKEN

SERVES 4

4 chicken breast fillets
1 large freezer bag
1 cup plain double-cream yoghurt
2 Tbsp chopped garlic
2 Tbsp sriracha sauce
½ cup chopped fresh herbs (parsley, basil, coriander, mint), plus extra, to garnish
Salt and pepper, to taste
1 Tbsp oil

1. Place the chicken breasts inside the freezer bag. Use a rolling pin or mallet to gently pound the chicken until each breast is evenly flattened.
2. To the bag, add the yoghurt, garlic, sriracha, herbs, and salt and pepper. Seal the bag and massage it to mix and distribute the marinade. Place the bag in the fridge and leave to marinate for at least 30 minutes, or overnight.
3. Heat a frying pan or griddle pan and add the oil. Fry the chicken until cooked through and golden on each side and. Garnish with fresh herbs and serve with a salad.

CREAMY COCONUT & CHICKPEA CHICKEN

SERVES 4

8 chicken pieces, bone-in and skin-on
2 Tbsp lemon pepper
1 Tbsp garlic powder
Salt and pepper, to taste
3 Tbsp olive oil
2 onions, sliced
1 Tbsp chopped garlic
1 Tbsp chopped ginger
Fresh chilli, chopped, to taste
1 can (400 g) chickpeas, drained and rinsed
1 chicken stock cube
1 can (400 ml) coconut milk
½ cup water
30 g fresh coriander, chopped

1. Preheat the oven to 200 °C.
2. Season the chicken pieces with lemon pepper, garlic powder, and salt and pepper.
3. Heat an ovenproof pot or pan over medium heat, add 2 tablespoons of olive oil and brown the chicken pieces (they don't need to be fully cooked at this stage). Remove from the pot and set aside.
4. In the same pot, heat the remaining olive oil. Add the onions and sauté until they've softened and started to brown around the edges. Stir in the garlic, ginger and chilli, and sauté for 1 minute.
5. Add the chickpeas and crumble in the stock cube. Stir in the coconut milk and water. Bring to a boil, then return the chicken pieces to the pot.
6. Place the pot, uncovered, into the oven to roast for 45 minutes, until the chicken is golden and cooked through, and the sauce has thickened. Stir in the fresh coriander just before serving. Serve with rice or crusty bread to soak up all of the delicious sauce.

CHICKEN CURRY

SERVES 6–8

3 Tbsp olive oil
2 onions, sliced
3 Tbsp chopped ginger
3 Tbsp chopped garlic
3 Tbsp Zola's Feasts Fragrant Curry Powder
1 medium carrot, peeled and finely chopped
1 × 1.5 kg whole chicken, cut into small pieces (or use chicken pieces of the same weight)
3 Tbsp Zola's Feasts Flavourbomb Spice Mix
± 1 cup water
4 potatoes, peeled and halved
Salt, to taste

1. Heat a pot over medium heat. Add the olive oil, onions, ginger and garlic, and sauté until the onions have softened. Add the Fragrant Curry Powder and carrot, and sauté for another 2 minutes.
2. Stir in the chicken pieces and Flavourbomb Spice Mix, then cover with a lid and allow the chicken to brown for 4 minutes. Stir occasionally to prevent burning, and add a splash of water if the spices are catching on the bottom of the pot.
3. Add the potatoes, season with salt, then add the rest of the water. Cover and leave to simmer gently over low heat until the potatoes are cooked through. (When the potatoes are cooked, the chicken should be cooked, too.)

BUTTER CHICKEN & PRAWN CURRY

SERVES 4–6

FOR THE MARINADE

½ cup plain double-cream yoghurt
1 Tbsp crushed garlic
1 Tbsp grated ginger
1 tsp chopped fresh chilli
1 tsp turmeric
2 tsp garam masala
1 tsp ground cumin
1 tsp salt
4 chicken breasts, cut into chunks
250 g peeled and deveined prawns

FOR THE SAUCE

2 Tbsp butter
1 onion, grated
2 Tbsp crushed garlic
1 Tbsp grated ginger
1 tsp ground coriander
1½ tsp ground cumin
1½ tsp garam masala
1 tsp chilli powder
1 can (410 g) puréed tomatoes
1 Tbsp sugar
1 cup pouring cream
Salt and pepper, to taste
2 Tbsp chopped fresh coriander

1. Mix together all the marinade ingredients (except the chicken and prawns) until well combined. Add the chicken and prawns and toss until evenly coated. Set aside to marinate while you make the sauce. You can do this the day before and leave to marinate overnight.
2. To make the sauce, add the butter to a pot and melt over medium heat. Add the onion, garlic and ginger, and sauté until softened. Stir in the coriander, cumin, garam masala and chilli powder, and sauté over low heat for 2 minutes to toast the spices. Stir in the puréed tomatoes and sugar, and simmer over low heat for 15 minutes.
3. Skewer the prawns onto sosatie sticks (I find it easier to cook them this way), then cook on a hot griddle pan until charred on the edges. Remove the prawns from the pan, then remove from the sosatie sticks and set aside. Next, cook the chicken pieces in the same griddle pan, until the edges are just charred.
4. Stir the cream into the sauce and simmer for another 5 minutes. Add the cooked prawns and chicken to the sauce and continue simmering until cooked through. Season with salt and pepper, and stir in the chopped coriander.

KORMA CHICKEN CURRY

SERVES 4–6

FOR THE MARINADE

½ cup plain double-cream yoghurt
2 tsp garam masala
1 tsp mild curry powder
1 tsp chilli powder
1 tsp salt
500 g skinless and boneless chicken thighs

FOR THE SAUCE

2 Tbsp oil
1 onion, grated
2 Tbsp crushed garlic
1 Tbsp grated ginger
1 tsp ground coriander
1½ tsp ground cumin
1½ tsp garam masala
½ tsp turmeric
2 fresh tomatoes, puréed (or grated)
1 Tbsp sugar
½ cup water
½ cup salted cashew nuts, finely ground
½ cup fresh cream
Salt and pepper, to taste
2 Tbsp chopped fresh coriander
¼ cup toasted cashew nuts, to garnish

1. Mix together all the marinade ingredients (except the chicken) until well combined. Add the chicken, toss well to coat and set aside to marinate while you make the sauce. You can do this the day before and leave to marinate overnight.
2. Heat a pot over medium heat. Add the oil, onion, garlic and ginger, and sauté until softened.
3. Stir in the coriander, cumin, garam masala and turmeric, and sauté over low heat for 2 minutes to toast the spices.
4. Stir in the chicken and any remaining marinade. Sauté over medium heat for 5 minutes.
5. Add the tomatoes, sugar and water. Lower the heat and simmer for 15 minutes.
6. Stir in the cashew nuts and cream, and simmer for another 20 minutes. Season with salt and pepper, and add the chopped coriander before serving. Garnish with the toasted cashews.

SPICED ROAST CHICKEN

SERVES 4–6

1 Tbsp ground coriander
1 Tbsp ground cumin
1 tsp paprika
1 Tbsp dried origanum
Salt and pepper, to taste
3 Tbsp olive oil
1 Tbsp Dijon mustard
2 kg whole chicken

1. Preheat the oven to 200 °C.
2. Combine the coriander, cumin, paprika, origanum, salt and pepper, olive oil and mustard. Rub the mixture all over the chicken.
3. Place the chicken in a roasting dish and cook, breast-side down, for 1 hour, then turn the chicken and cook for another 40 minutes. Remove from the oven, tent with foil and leave to rest for at least 20 minutes before carving.

BACON, CHICKEN & CORN CHOWDER

SERVES 4

2 Tbsp olive oil
1 onion, chopped
150 g bacon, diced
2 garlic cloves, chopped
½ tsp dried chilli flakes
1 tsp paprika
1 Tbsp cake flour
1 potato, peeled and cut into chunks
1 can (415 g) creamed sweetcorn
1½ cups vegetable stock
1 ½ cups milk
½ cup fresh cream
2 (± 150 g total) chicken breast fillets, diced
Salt and pepper, to taste
2 Tbsp chopped parsley

1. Heat a large pot and add the olive oil, onion, and bacon. Sauté until the onion begins to soften. Add the garlic, chilli flakes, paprika and flour, and sauté for another minute.
2. Stir in the potato, creamed sweetcorn, stock and milk. Cover with a lid and simmer for 20 minutes, or until the potatoes are cooked through.
3. Add the cream and chicken, and season with salt and pepper. Simmer for 5–8 minutes, or until the chicken is cooked through. Stir in the chopped parsley before serving.

SAUCY LAMB CHOPS & PEPPERS

SERVES 4

8 lamb loin chops
3 Tbsp Zola's Feasts Flavourbomb Spice Mix
2 Tbsp olive oil
1 each red and orange pepper, pith removed, and diced
2 garlic cloves, chopped
½ cup sweet chilli sauce or fruit chutney
¼ cup water
Salt, to taste

1. Season the lamb chops on both sides with the Flavourbomb Spice Mix.
2. Heat a pan over high heat and add the olive oil. Brown the chops on each side (they don't have to be fully cooked at this stage). Remove from the pan and set aside.
3. Add the red and orange peppers to the pan and sauté until softened. Add the garlic and sauté for another minute. Stir in the chilli sauce (or chutney) and water, and bring to a boil.
4. Return the chops to the pan and allow them to simmer in the sauce until the sauce has thickened and the chops are cooked to your liking. Season with salt. Serve with rice, mash, veggies or any accompaniment of your choice.

SPICED LAMB RIBS

SERVES 4

1 Tbsp cumin seeds
1 tsp coriander seeds
1 tsp fennel seeds
1 tsp dried chilli flakes
½ tsp whole black peppercorns
1 tsp salt
¼ cup olive oil
12 individual lamb ribs

1. Prepare some coals for the braai.
2. Grind the cumin seeds, coriander seeds, fennel seeds, chilli flakes, peppercorns and salt with a pestle and mortar until coarse. Mix in the olive oil, then rub the mixture all over the lamb ribs.
3. Braai the ribs over hot coals until crisp and cooked through.

CURRIED LAMB SHANKS

SERVES 4

4 lamb shanks
Salt and pepper, to taste
3 Tbsp olive oil
2 onions, sliced
1 dried chilli
(or ½ tsp dried chilli flakes)
1 star anise
2 cardamom pods
3 sprigs fresh thyme
3 garlic cloves, chopped
2 tsp ginger paste
2 tsp ground cumin
1 Tbsp ground coriander
1 tsp chilli powder
2 Tbsp Zola's Feasts
Fragrant Curry Powder
300 g cherry tomatoes (or regular
tomatoes), puréed or chopped
600 ml lamb or beef stock

1. Season the lamb shanks with salt and pepper.
2. Heat a pot and add the oil. Add the shanks and brown on high heat until golden on all sides. Remove from the pot and set aside.
3. To the same pot, add the onions, dried chilli, star anise, cardamom and thyme. Cook over medium heat, until the onions are soft and caramelised.
4. Lower the heat and add the garlic, ginger paste, cumin, coriander, chilli powder, and curry powder. Gently cook the onions and spices for 6–8 minutes, stirring occasionally. Stir in the tomatoes and stock, then bring to a boil.
5. Return the lamb shanks to the pot. Cover with a lid and simmer over low heat for 3–4 hours, until the sauce has thickened and the meat is tender and falling off the bone. (You can also cook the shanks in the oven at 160 °C for 3–4 hours).

HEARTY OXTAIL

SERVES 4–6

1 kg oxtail
¼ cup flour
Salt and pepper, to taste
2 Tbsp olive oil
2 onions, chopped
2 carrots, peeled and diced
2 bay leaves
4 sprigs fresh thyme
1 Tbsp Zola's Feasts Fragrant Curry Powder
2 Tbsp tomato paste
1 can (410 g) chopped tomatoes
2 Tbsp sugar
4 cups beef stock

1. Dust the oxtail in flour and salt and pepper.
2. Heat a pot and add the olive oil. Add the oxtail in batches and brown on all sides. Remove from the pot and set aside.
3. To the same pot, add the onions, carrots, bay leaves and thyme. Sauté until the vegetables begin to soften and brown.
4. Add the Fragrant Curry Powder and tomato paste, and cook for another minute. Stir in the chopped tomatoes, sugar and stock, and bring to a simmer.
5. Return the oxtail to the pot. Cover with a lid and simmer gently over low heat for 3½ hours, until the sauce has thickened and the meat is tender and falling off the bone.

BEEF PHYLLO POT PIE

SERVES 4–6

3 Tbsp olive oil
1 kg stewing beef
Salt and pepper, to taste
1 onion, chopped
2 carrots, peeled and chopped
500 g butternut, peeled and chopped
3 bay leaves
2 garlic cloves, chopped
4 sprigs fresh thyme
1 tsp dried chilli flakes
¼ cup cake flour
2 Tbsp tomato paste
1 tsp sugar (or to taste)
2 cups beef stock
8 sheets phyllo pastry, defrosted
100 g butter, melted

1. Heat an ovenproof pan and add 2 tablespoons of olive oil. Add the beef and brown over high heat. Season with salt and pepper, then remove the beef from the pan and set aside.
2. Add the remaining olive oil to the same pan, along with the onion, carrots and butternut. Sauté for a few minutes over medium heat, then stir in the bay leaves, garlic, thyme and chilli flakes. Add the flour and tomato paste, stir to coat the veggies and cook for a couple of minutes.
3. Return the beef to the pan, add the sugar and beef stock and stir well. Bring to a boil, then lower the heat. Cover with a lid and simmer for 1 hour, or until the meat is tender. Taste for seasoning.
4. Preheat the oven to 180 °C. Scrunch each sheet of pastry in your hands, then place them directly onto the stew to cover. Brush the top with melted butter, then bake in the oven for 20–30 minutes until crisp and golden brown.

BEEF SHIN & GREEN BEAN STEW

SERVES 4–6

2 Tbsp olive oil
2 kg beef shin, bone-in
1 onion, chopped
2 carrots, peeled and chopped
1 Tbsp chopped fresh thyme
1 Tbsp chopped fresh origanum
1 Tbsp chopped garlic
1 Tbsp paprika
1 tsp cayenne pepper
2 Tbsp tomato paste
1 beef stock cube
3 cups water
1 Tbsp sugar
Salt and pepper, to taste
150 g green beans, trimmed

1. Heat a pot over high heat and add the olive oil. Add the beef and cook until browned. You might need to do this in batches, depending on the size of your pot.
2. Add the onion, carrots, thyme and origanum, and sauté until the onion has softened.
3. Stir in the garlic, paprika, cayenne pepper and tomato paste, and cook for 2 minutes. Add the stock cube and water and bring to a simmer. Cover with a lid and cook over low heat for 1½ hours, or until the beef is tender. (You might need to top up the water while cooking so the stew doesn't dry out.) Once the beef is tender, add the sugar and season with salt and pepper.
4. Add the green beans and simmer for another 5 minutes, or until the beans are cooked but still slightly crisp.

BEEF & BARLEY STEW

SERVES 4

2 Tbsp olive oil
500 g stewing beef
1 onion, chopped
2 carrots, peeled and chopped
2 tsp paprika
1 tsp dried thyme
2 tsp crushed garlic and ginger
1 cup pearl barley
1 stock cube dissolved in
  4 cups hot water
Salt and pepper, to taste
2 Tbsp chopped fresh parsley

1. Heat a large pot and add the olive oil and beef. Sauté on high heat until the meat has browned.
2. Add the onion and carrots, then lower the heat to medium and sauté for 5 minutes. Stir in the paprika, thyme, and garlic and ginger paste.
3. Stir in the pearl barley and stock. Cover with a lid and simmer for 1½ hours over low heat, checking every 30 minutes to top up the water if necessary.
4. Once the barley is cooked through and the meat is tender, season with salt and pepper. Stir in the parsley before serving.

CURRIED MINCE

SERVES 4

2 Tbsp canola oil
1 onion, chopped
1 Tbsp chopped garlic
500 g beef mince
2 Tbsp Zola's Feasts Fragrant Curry Powder
1 tomato, chopped
2 cups beef stock
2 potatoes, peeled and chopped
Salt and pepper, to taste
Fresh coriander, chopped, to garnish

1. Heat a pot over medium heat. Add the oil, onion and garlic, and sauté for 5–6 minutes, or until the onion has softened.
2. Add the beef mince and fry until browned, stirring to break up the meat.
3. Stir in the Fragrant Curry Powder and tomato, and cook for a few minutes.
4. Stir in the stock and potatoes, cover with a lid and simmer for 30 minutes. Season with salt and pepper, and garnish with coriander. Serve with roti.

LASAGNE

SERVES 6–8

FOR THE MEAT SAUCE

3 Tbsp olive oil
1 onion, chopped
1 carrot, peeled and grated
2 garlic cloves, finely chopped
500 g lean beef mince
2 Tbsp dried origanum
2 Tbsp tomato paste
1 Tbsp sugar
1 can (410 g) chopped tomatoes
1 beef stock cube
1 cup water
Salt and pepper, to taste

FOR THE CHEESE SAUCE

80 g butter
¼ cup flour
3 cups milk
200 g cheddar cheese, grated
Salt and pepper, to taste

TO ASSEMBLE

9 uncooked lasagne sheets (depending on the number of layers desired)

1. To make the meat sauce, heat a pot over medium heat. Add the olive oil, onion, carrot and garlic, and sauté until the veggies begin to soften. Add the mince and origanum, and sauté until the mince begins to brown.
2. Stir in the tomato paste and sugar, then sauté for 1 minute. Add the chopped tomatoes, stock cube and water, cover with a lid and simmer over low heat for 30 minutes, stirring occasionally. Season with salt and pepper.
3. To make the cheese sauce, melt the butter in a saucepan, whisk in the flour and cook for 1 minute. Whisk in the milk and keep stirring until the sauce thickens and bubbles. Simmer for 5 minutes. Stir in ¾ of the grated cheese and season to taste.

4. Preheat the oven to 180 °C. Spoon a third of the meat sauce into the bottom of a baking dish, then top with a layer of lasagne sheets, followed by a third of the cheese sauce. Sprinkle over some of the remaining grated cheese. Repeat this process until you have three layers, ending with a layer of cheese sauce and a sprinkle of grated cheese.
5. Bake the lasagne in the oven for 30 minutes, until the cheese on top is melted and golden, and the lasagne sheets in the centre are cooked through.

HONEY-MUSTARD PORK ROAST

SERVES 4

1 kg pork rump roast
Salt and pepper, to taste
2 Tbsp canola oil
1 cup orange juice
2 Tbsp wholegrain mustard
2 Tbsp honey
Pinch dried chilli flakes (optional)
2 garlic cloves, chopped

1. Preheat the oven to 180 °C. Season the pork with salt and pepper.
2. Heat an ovenproof pan over high heat and add the oil. Sear the pork on all sides until golden (it doesn't have to be fully cooked at this stage).
3. Whisk together the orange juice, mustard, honey, chilli flakes and garlic. Pour the mixture over the pork, cover with foil and roast for 1 hour.
4. Remove the roast from the oven, baste with the juices, cover with foil and return to the oven for another 20 minutes.
5. Remove the roast from the oven, baste again, cover with foil then leave to rest for 30 minutes before slicing and serving. Serve any extra juices on the side as a sauce.

RED

USHATINI (RAW SALSA)

SERVES 4

4 ripe tomatoes, diced
½ onion, finely chopped
Fresh green chilli, sliced, to taste
½ tsp salt
1 Tbsp white vinegar

1. Combine all the ingredients in a bowl and toss well to mix.

USHATINI (COOKED SALSA)

SERVES 4

2 Tbsp olive oil
1 onion, finely chopped
Fresh chilli, chopped, to taste
1 Tbsp curry powder
6 ripe tomatoes, diced
½ stock cube (vegetable, chicken or beef)
Salt, to taste

1. Heat a pot and add the olive oil. Add the onion and sauté until softened. Add the chilli and curry powder, then sauté for 1 minute.
2. Add the tomatoes and crumble in the stock cube. Lower the heat and simmer gently for 20 minutes, until the tomatoes have broken down and the sauce has reduced. Season with salt.

USHATINI (RAW SALSA)

SERVING SUGGESTION

Add sliced green beans or baby marrows. Simmer the vegetables for 4 minutes to cook before serving.

USHATINI
(COOKED SALSA)

MARINATED TOMATO SALAD

SERVES 4

1 tsp Dijon mustard
1 tsp honey
Juice of ½ lemon
¼ cup extra-virgin olive oil
2 Tbsp chopped fresh parsley
1 punnet (250 g) cherry tomatoes, halved
Salt and pepper, to taste

1. Whisk together the mustard, honey, lemon juice, olive oil and parsley.
2. Add the tomatoes, season with salt and pepper, and toss well. Leave to stand for 10 minutes before serving, to allow the flavours to develop.

MARINATED
TOMATO SALAD

BEETROOT
WITH PEPPADEW® & BALSAMIC DRESSING

SERVES 4–6

1 kg whole beetroot
6 cups cold water
Pinch salt
6 Peppadews®, finely chopped (plus 2 Tbsp Peppadew® preserving liquid)
1 tsp Dijon mustard
3 Tbsp honey
¼ cup balsamic vinegar
¼ cup extra-virgin olive oil
Salt and pepper, to taste

1. Wash the beetroot well, then add to a pot and cover with the cold water. Add the salt, bring to a boil and cook 1 hour, or until fork tender. Allow to cool, then peel and dice.
2. In a bowl, whisk together the chopped Peppadews® and preserving liquid, Dijon mustard, honey and balsamic vinegar until well combined. While whisking, slowly add the olive oil so that the dressing emulsifies. Season with salt and pepper.
3. Toss the diced beetroot in the dressing until evenly coated.

TOMATO & GINGER SMOOR

SERVES 4

2 Tbsp olive oil
2 onions, finely chopped
¼ cup chopped ginger
Pinch dried chilli flakes
1 tsp ground ginger
4 tomatoes, diced
¼ cup sugar
2 Tbsp white wine vinegar
1 tsp salt

1. Heat a pan over medium heat and add the olive oil. Add the onion and sauté until translucent. Stir in the chopped ginger, chilli flakes and ground ginger, and sauté for 1 minute.
2. Stir in the tomatoes, sugar, vinegar and salt, and sauté for another 10 minutes, until the tomatoes have broken down.

EGG CHUTNEY

SERVES 4

Water, for boiling
8 large eggs
2 Tbsp olive oil
1 onion, sliced
1 Tbsp chopped ginger
1 Tbsp chopped garlic
1 tsp chilli powder
1 Tbsp Zola's Feasts Fragrant Curry Powder
2 Tbsp tomato paste
1 can (400 g) chopped tomatoes
2 tsp sugar
Salt, to taste
2 Tbsp chopped fresh coriander

1. Bring a pot of water to a boil, add the eggs and simmer for 8 minutes. Then, remove the eggs from the boiling water and plunge into cold water for about 5 minutes. Once they are cool to the touch, peel the eggs and set them aside.
2. Heat a saucepan over medium heat and add the olive oil. Add the onion, ginger and garlic, and sauté until the onion softens and starts to brown around the edges.
3. Lower the heat and add the chilli powder and curry powder. Sauté for a minute. Add the tomato paste and continue to cook over low heat for a couple of minutes. Stir in the chopped tomatoes and sugar, then season with salt. Cover with a lid and simmer for 5 minutes.
4. Add the boiled eggs to the chutney and simmer for 2 minutes. Stir in the coriander and serve with rice.

CHILLI-SESAME SALMON

SERVES 4

- 2 Tbsp gochujang paste (Korean chilli paste)
- 2 Tbsp soy sauce
- 1 Tbsp sesame oil
- ½ Tbsp fish sauce
- 2 tsp sugar
- 1 Tbsp sesame seeds
- 4 × 150 g skinless salmon fillets
- 2 Tbsp vegetable oil

1. In a bowl, whisk together the gochujang paste, soy sauce, sesame oil, fish sauce, sugar and sesame seeds.
2. Add the salmon fillets and coat well in the marinade. Leave to marinate for a few hours, or overnight.
3. Heat a hot griddle pan over medium heat and add the oil. Sear the salmon for about 2 minutes on each side (or longer, if you prefer your salmon more well-done).

A RAINBOW OF COLOURS

RAINBOW COLESLAW

SERVES 4

2 cups shredded green cabbage
1 cup shredded red cabbage
1 cup coarsely grated carrot
½ onion, finely chopped
3 Tbsp chopped parsley
1 cup plain yoghurt
1 cup mayonnaise
2 Tbsp honey
2 Tbsp white wine vinegar

1. Combine all the ingredients in a large bowl. Mix well until all the ingredients are well combined and evenly coated.

SAVOURY
MEALIE RICE
MEALIE RICE SALAD

SAVOURY MEALIE RICE

SERVES 4

2 Tbsp olive oil
1 onion, chopped
½ each red and green pepper, pith removed, and diced
2 garlic cloves, chopped
1½ Tbsp Zola's Feasts Flavourbomb Spice Mix
150 g mushrooms, sliced
1 cup mealie (maize) rice, rinsed and drained
1 cup whole kernel sweetcorn
2 cups chicken stock
Salt and pepper, to taste

1. Heat a pan over medium heat and add the olive oil. Add the onion, peppers and garlic, and sauté until softened. Add the Flavourbomb Spice Mix and mushrooms, and sauté for another minute.
2. Stir in the mealie rice until evenly coated in the spices. Pour in the chicken stock and add the corn. Cover with a lid and simmer gently for 30–40 minutes, or until the mealie rice has absorbed the stock and is cooked through.
3. After cooking, use a fork to fluff the rice. Season with salt and pepper.

MEALIE RICE SALAD

SERVES 4

1 cup mealie (maize) rice
Cold water
½ tsp salt
1 tsp wholegrain mustard
2 spring onions, chopped
Juice of 1 lemon
1 Tbsp honey
2 Tbsp chopped fresh coriander
4 Tbsp olive oil
½ punnet (125 g) cherry tomatoes, chopped
1 cup chopped cucumber
Salt and pepper, to taste

1. Rinse the mealie rice under cold water, then add to a pot. Cover with more cold water, add the salt and bring to a boil. Simmer over medium heat for 40 minutes, topping up the water if necessary, until the mealie rice is cooked through and tender. Drain the rice in a colander and set aside to cool.
2. Mix the wholegrain mustard, spring onions, lemon juice, honey, coriander and olive oil in a large bowl. Add the cherry tomatoes and cucumber, then fold in the cooked mealie rice. Season with salt and pepper.

CHAKALAKA RICE

SERVES 4

2 cups boiling water
1 cup basmati rice
2 Tbsp olive oil
1 onion, chopped
½ each red and green pepper, pith removed, and diced
1 Tbsp chopped garlic
2 tsp chopped ginger
Pinch dried chilli flakes
3 Tbsp Zola's Feasts Fragrant Curry Powder
2 carrots, peeled and grated
2½ cups vegetable stock
1 can (410 g) baked beans
Salt and pepper, to taste
Fresh coriander, to serve

1. Pour the boiling water over the basmati rice and set aside to soak for 30 minutes, before straining in a colander.
2. Heat a large pan over medium heat and add the olive oil. Add the onion, peppers, garlic and ginger, and sauté until softened.
3. Stir in the chilli flakes and Fragrant Curry Powder, and sauté over low heat for 1 minute to cook the spices. Add the carrots and drained rice, and stir to coat evenly in the spices.
4. Stir in the stock and baked beans, and season with salt and pepper. Cover with a lid, then simmer over medium heat for 10 minutes.
5. Turn off the heat, leave the lid on and allow to stand for another 10 minutes. Use a fork to fluff and separate the grains of rice. Serve with fresh coriander.

CHAKALAKA

SERVES 4

2 Tbsp oil
1 onion, diced
½ red pepper, pith removed, and diced
¼ each yellow and green pepper, pith removed, and diced
2 garlic cloves, chopped
1 Tbsp grated ginger
2 Tbsp Zola's Feasts Fragrant Curry Powder
2 carrots, grated
1 can (410 g) baked beans
½ cup water
Salt and pepper, to taste

1. Heat a pan over medium heat and add the oil. Add the onion, peppers, garlic and ginger, and sauté until soft.
2. Stir in the Fragrant Curry Powder and sauté for a minute.
3. Add the carrots and baked beans, and stir. Pour in the water, cover with a lid and simmer for 5 minutes before serving.

RICE-STUFFED BRINJALS
WITH TOMATO SALSA & TAHINI-YOGHURT SAUCE

SERVES 2 AS A MAIN OR 4 AS A STARTER

FOR THE STUFFED BRINJALS
2 brinjals
Salt and pepper, to taste
Olive oil, for drizzling, + 2 Tbsp
1 Tbsp cumin seeds
½ tsp dried chilli flakes (or to taste)
1 onion, chopped
2 garlic cloves, finely chopped
½ each yellow and red pepper, pith removed, and diced
2 cups cooked rice
1 cup cottage cheese
100 g feta cheese, crumbled

FOR THE TOMATO SALSA
1 punnet (250 g) cherry tomatoes, quartered
1 Tbsp each chopped fresh parsley, basil and mint

FOR THE SAUCE
2 Tbsp tahini paste
½ cup plain yoghurt
Juice of 2 lemons
Lemon wedges, to serve

1. Preheat the oven to 180 °C.
2. To make the brinjals, cut the them in half lengthways. Use a sharp knife to score the flesh in a crisscross pattern. Place the halved brinjals into a roasting dish, flesh-side up. Season with salt and pepper, then drizzle with olive oil. Cover the dish with foil and place in the oven to roast for about 30–40 minutes, or until tender (the roasting time will depend on the size of the brinjals). Once cooked, remove the brinjals from the oven and set aside to cool.
3. Heat a pan over medium heat, then add 2 tablespoons of olive oil, the cumin seeds, chilli flakes, onion, garlic and peppers. Sauté until the veggies soften. Add the cooked rice and stir to combine.
4. Remove the pan from the heat. Add the cottage cheese and most of the feta (reserve some for sprinkling on top). Season with salt and pepper.
5. Scoop the flesh from the brinjals, leaving a 1–2 mm border. Add the flesh to the rice mixture and mix well, then spoon the mixture back into the brinjal skins and sprinkle with the reserved feta. Return the brinjals to the oven for another 20 minutes, or until heated through.
7. To make the salsa, combine the cherry tomatoes, parsley, basil and mint, salt and pepper, and a drizzle of olive oil.

8. To make the sauce, combine the tahini and yoghurt with enough lemon juice to get a pouring consistency. Season to taste.
9. Spoon the salsa over the brinjals and drizzle with the sauce. Serve with lemon wedges.

MINESTRONE

SERVES 4

2 Tbsp olive oil
1 onion, diced
2 garlic cloves, chopped
½ red chilli, chopped (optional)
1 bay leaf
2 carrots, peeled and diced
1 can (410 g) chopped tomatoes
2 tsp sugar
3 cups vegetable stock
½ cup pasta rice
4 baby marrows, diced
1 cup chopped green beans
Salt and pepper, to taste
2 Tbsp each chopped basil and Italian flat-leaf parsley

1. Heat a large pot over medium heat. Add the olive oil and onion, and sauté until softened. Stir in the garlic, chilli (if using), bay leaf and carrots, and sauté for 1 minute.
2. Stir in the chopped tomatoes, sugar and vegetable stock. Cover with a lid and simmer for 10 minutes.
3. Add the pasta rice, baby marrows and green beans. Season with salt and pepper. Cover again and simmer for 5–7 minutes, or until the pasta rice is cooked. Stir in the basil and parsley, and serve.

MINCE & CHUNKY VEG STEW

SERVES 4–6

2 Tbsp olive oil
500 g beef mince
1 onion, chopped
1 Tbsp flour
1 Tbsp chopped garlic
1 Tbsp dried origanum
Pinch dried chilli flakes
1 Tbsp barbecue spice
1 beef stock cube
4 cups water
150 g butternut, peeled and chopped
2 potatoes, peeled and chopped
2 cups chopped spinach

1. Heat a pot over medium heat and add the olive oil. Stir in the beef mince and onion, and cook until browned. Add the flour and stir to coat the mince.
2. Add the garlic, origanum, chilli flakes and barbecue spice, and sauté for a few minutes.
3. Crumble in the stock cube, add the water and bring to a boil. Stir in the butternut and potatoes, then cover with a lid and simmer for 1 hour.
4. After 1 hour, add the spinach and cook for another 10 minutes.

FISH PAELLA

SERVES 4

1 lemon
Fish fillets (200 g per person, any firm white fish)
2 tsp smoked paprika
1 Tbsp dried origanum
Salt and pepper, to taste
2 Tbsp olive oil
1 onion, diced
¼ each red, yellow and green peppers, pith removed, and diced
100 g chorizo sausage, sliced
2 Tbsp chopped garlic
1½ cups short-grain white rice
1 vegetable stock cube
3 cups water

1. Squeeze the juice of half the lemon over the fish fillets. Sprinkle the fillets with a pinch of paprika and a pinch of **origanum**, and season with salt and pepper. Set aside.
2. Heat a pan over medium heat. Add the olive oil, onion, peppers, chorizo and garlic. Sauté until the veggies soften.
3. Add the remaining paprika and **origanum**, as well as the rice. Sauté for 2 minutes to toast the rice.
4. Add the vegetable stock cube and 2 cups of water. Bring to a boil, then cover with a lid and simmer for about 10 minutes, until the water is absorbed.
5. Place the fish fillets on top of the rice and vegetables and add the remaining cup of water. Cover again and simmer for 10–15 minutes more, until the fish is flaky and the rice is cooked through. Season with salt and pepper and a squeeze of lemon juice.

CURRIED PORK CHOPS

SERVES 4

4 × 200 g pork chops
2 Tbsp Zola's Feasts Fragrant Curry Powder
Salt, to taste
2 Tbsp olive oil
1 each red and yellow pepper, pith removed, and roughly chopped
½ cup water
1 cup fresh cream
Fresh coriander, to serve

1. Sprinkle the pork chops with 1 tablespoon of the Fragrant Curry Powder and season with salt.
2. Heat a pan over medium heat and add the olive oil. Fry the pork chops until golden on each side, then remove from the pan and set aside.
3. To the same pan, add the peppers and remaining curry powder. Sauté until softened.
4. Deglaze the pan with the water, then add the cream and bring to a simmer.
5. Return the pork chops to the pan, cover with a lid and continue to simmer for 5 minutes, or until the chops are cooked through. Season to taste and stir in the fresh coriander before serving.

AFTERS (DESSERT)

RAISIN SCONES

MAKES 12

4 cups cake flour
20 ml baking powder
120 g cold butter, diced
1 cup white sugar
1 cup raisins
4 large eggs
240 ml amasi (or buttermilk)
1 tsp vanilla extract

1. Preheat the oven to 180 °C.
2. In a bowl, sift together the flour and baking powder, then rub in the cold butter until the mixture resembles breadcrumbs. Stir in the sugar and raisins.
3. In a separate bowl, whisk together the eggs, amasi and vanilla extract.
4. Pour half the amasi and egg mixture into the dry-ingredient mixture, then fold gently with a palette knife (or butter knife). Add more of the Amasi and egg mixture, a little at a time, while continuing to mix gently, until the mixture comes together to form a dough.
5. Use your hands to gently knead the dough until it comes together. Turn it out onto a floured surface, use a rolling pin or your hands to flatten it out to about 2 cm thick, then cut out rounds using a cutter dusted with flour.
6. Gather any remaining dough, knead, flatten and continue to cut it into rounds until there is no more dough left. Place the rounds onto a lined baking tray, brush the tops with any remaining amasi and egg mixture or with some milk. Bake for 20–25 minutes or until the scones are golden.

PEACHES & CREAM BOMBE

SERVES 8–10

100 g Christmas fruit pudding
1 can (410 g) sliced peaches, drained (reserve the liquid)
1 kg vanilla ice cream, softened and divided
100 g white chocolate, melted

1. Line a dome-shaped bowl (about 20–24 cm) with cling wrap, then set aside.
2. Purée the sliced peaches and set aside.
3. Crumble the fruit pudding into a separate bowl, then mix in ¼ cup of the peach liquid.
4. Press the pudding mixture into the lined bowl. (The bottom and sides of the bowl will form the outer layer of the domed pudding, so make sure there are no gaps.)
5. Press half the vanilla ice cream into the bowl until it is half-full. Place it in the freezer for 30 minutes to set.
6. Mix the puréed peaches into the remaining ice cream. Spoon the mixture into the pudding, on top of the other ice cream layer. Freeze for at least 4 hours, or until completely set.
7. Once set, turn out the pudding from its bowl onto a serving platter and peel off the cling wrap. Drizzle the pudding with melted white chocolate to decorate, then store in the freezer until ready to serve.
8. To serve, remove the pudding from the freezer 10 minutes before serving and slice into wedges.

CREAM DOUGHNUTS

MAKES 12

2 cups flour
10 g instant dry yeast
¼ cup sugar
½ tsp salt
1 egg
½ cup milk
± ½ cup water
Oil, for frying
1 cup castor sugar, for coating
2 cups whipping cream
½ cup icing sugar
2 tsp vanilla extract

1. Mix together the flour, yeast, sugar and salt in a bowl.
2. In a separate bowl, whisk together the egg and milk, then add to the dry ingredients. Mix well, adding enough water to form a pliable dough.
3. Knead the dough for 10 minutes, or until smooth. Cover with a damp cloth or cling wrap and leave to rise until it has doubled in size.
4. Divide the dough into 12 pieces and shape them into long doughnuts. Place them on a floured tray, cover again and leave to rise for 10 minutes.
5. Place 8–10 cm of oil in a pot and heat to 170 °C. Use a candy (sugar) thermometer to measure the oil temperature. Alternatively, sprinkle some flour into the oil – if it sizzles and browns, the oil is ready for frying. Deep-fry each doughnut until golden all over. Drain on paper towel, then coat in castor sugar before allowing to cool completely.
6. Combine the whipping cream, icing sugar and vanilla extract, then whip to stiff peaks. Place the cream mixture into a piping bag. Cut a slit in each cooled doughnut and pipe with the cream mixture.

MILK TART SPRING ROLLS

MAKES 8–12

2 cups milk
2 egg yolks
½ cup castor sugar
2 Tbsp flour
2 Tbsp cornflour
1 tsp vanilla extract
1 tsp ground cinnamon
12 spring roll wrappers
1 egg white, lightly beaten
Oil, for frying

FOR COATING

¼ cup castor sugar
2 tsp ground cinnamon

1. Heat the milk to scalding point (just before it starts to boil).
2. In a bowl, whisk together the egg yolks, castor sugar, flour and cornflour. Pour the hot milk into the egg mixture, whisking continuously. Return the mixture to the pot and cook on medium heat until thickened, stirring continuously.
3. Stir in the vanilla extract and cinnamon. Transfer the mixture to a bowl, cover with cling wrap and leave to cool completely.
4. Once the mixture has cooled, spoon it onto the spring roll wrappers and roll them into neat cigars. Brush the edges with egg white to seal.
5. Deep-fry in oil (5 cm is enough) until golden and crisp. Drain them of excess oil on paper towel, then toss in a mixture of castor sugar and cinnamon to coat. Serve immediately.

ICE CREAM PUFFS

MAKES 8–12

FOR THE CHOUX PASTRY

1 cup water
1 cup milk
160 g cold butter, diced
2 cups cake flour
6 large eggs, lightly beaten

FOR THE FILLING

Vanilla ice cream
(or your favourite flavour)

Icing sugar, for dusting

1. Preheat the oven to 200 °C.
2. Place the water, milk and butter in a pot, cover with a lid and bring to a boil. As soon as the liquid begins to boil, add all the flour at once and stir until a dough forms. Cook the mixture for 1 minute, or until the dough starts to come away from the sides of the pot. Remove from the heat and set aside to cool slightly.
3. Once the dough is cool to the touch, slowly mix in the beaten eggs, a little at a time, mixing well after each addition. The dough should take on a smooth, dropping consistency.
4. Using a large serving spoon, dollop mounds of dough onto a greased baking tray. Make sure to leave some space between each one, as the puffs will get bigger in the oven.
5. Place the tray in the oven and bake for 20–25 minutes, or until puffed and golden.
6. Remove the puffs from the oven and pierce the bottom of each one with a skewer to allow the steam to escape. Return them to the oven for another 10 minutes to dry out the pastry. Then, allow to cool completely on a wire rack.
7. To serve, cut the puffs in half and fill each one with a scoop of ice cream. Dust with icing sugar.

STRAWBERRY UPSIDE-DOWN CAKE

FOR THE STRAWBERRIES

¼ cup castor sugar
¼ cup maple syrup
¼ cup butter, melted
Juice of 1 lemon
250 g fresh strawberries, sliced

FOR THE SPONGE

120 g butter, softened
120 g castor sugar
Zest of 1 lemon (use the same lemon from the strawberry mixture)
2 eggs
175 ml plain yoghurt
160 g cake flour
1 tsp baking powder
1 tsp bicarbonate of soda

Plain yoghurt and vanilla extract, to serve

1. Preheat the oven to 180 °C.
2. Line a 20 cm cake tin with greaseproof paper.
3. To make the strawberries, combine the castor sugar, maple syrup, melted butter, lemon juice and strawberries in a bowl. Spread the mixture over the bottom of the cake tin.
4. To make the sponge, cream the butter, castor sugar and lemon zest.
5. Whisk together the eggs and yoghurt.
6. Sift together the cake flour, baking powder and bicarbonate of soda.
7. Fold the dry and wet ingredients alternately into the creamed butter and sugar. Spoon the mixture carefully over the strawberries in the cake tin, then bake for 40–60 minutes, or until a skewer inserted into the centre comes out clean.
8. Remove from the oven and allow to cool in the tin for 10 minutes before turning out. Leave to cool completely, then serve with a dollop of plain yoghurt mixed with vanilla extract.

PEACH & AMASI ICE CREAM

SERVES 4–6

4 peaches (fresh or canned), chopped
¼ cup white sugar
¼ cup water
1 can (385 g) sweetened condensed milk
1 cup amasi
1 tsp vanilla extract
1 cup whipping cream

1. Add the peaches, sugar and water to a saucepan and cook over medium heat until the peaches soften. Remove from the heat, then purée until smooth. Set aside to cool.
2. Whip the cream to soft peaks. In a separate bowl, mix the condensed milk, amasi and vanilla extract until well combined. Stir in the whipped cream and half of the cooled peach purée. Pour the mixture into a freezer-proof dish. Drizzle the remaining purée over the ice cream, then swirl with a knife. Cover and freeze until set. Scoop and serve.

PEPPERMINT CRISP TART

SERVES 4–6

2 cups whipping cream
1 can (360 g) Nestlé Caramel Treat
2 × 200 g packets coconut biscuits, coarsely crushed
300 g Nestlé Peppermint Crisp chocolate, crushed

1. In a bowl, whip the cream to soft peaks.
2. In a separate bowl, whip the caramel until it is smooth, then fold in the whipped cream.
3. Layer half the crushed biscuits in a serving dish, then top with half the cream-caramel mixture. Sprinkle with half the crushed Peppermint Crisp chocolate, then top with another layer of biscuits. Top with another layer of the remaining cream-caramel mixture, then sprinkle with the rest of the Peppermint Crisp chocolate. Refrigerate until set.

BLACK FOREST MACARON STACK

(CAN ALSO BE MADE AS 24 SMALL, INDIVIDUAL MACARON SANDWICHES)

FOR THE MACARONS
200 g almond flour
450 g icing sugar, plus extra to decorate
50 g cocoa powder
8 large egg whites
220 g castor sugar

FOR THE FILLING
500 g plain cream cheese, room temperature
6 Tbsp icing sugar
1 tsp vanilla extract
1 cup cream, whipped
2 cans (2 × 425 g) preserved black cherries, drained

1. Draw three 18 cm circles on baking paper and place them onto the baking trays. Preheat the oven to 160 °C.
2. In a bowl, sift together the almond flour, icing sugar and cocoa powder. Set aside.
3. To make the meringue, in a separate, clean bowl, whisk the egg whites until soft peaks form, then gradually whisk in the castor sugar. Whip until stiff peaks form.
4. Fold the almond flour mixture into the meringue in three batches (this will prevent knocking too much air out of the meringue too quickly) to form a thick batter. Once all the almond flour mixture has been incorporated, continue mixing until the batter loosens and starts to run down the sides of the bowl.
5. Transfer the mixture to a piping bag fitted with a round nozzle. Pipe the mixture in concentric circles onto the three large baking-paper circles. Use the remaining mixture to pipe small individual macaron rounds, the size of a 50c coin, onto a separate sheet of baking paper and place onto a baking tray.
6. Bang the baking trays onto the work surface to get rid of any air bubbles and to flatten the macarons. Leave to stand at room temperature for 30 minutes, or until a skin forms.
7. Bake the large macarons for 25–30 minutes, and the smaller macarons for 15–20 minutes, until the tops have hardened and the macaron has sprung up from its base to form a foot (the bubbly bit that forms at the bottom of the macaron). Remove from the oven and leave to cool completely on the baking trays.
8. To make the filling, mix the cream cheese, icing sugar and vanilla extract until smooth. Whip the cream and fold into the mixture, then refrigerate for 30 minutes.
9. Place the filling into a piping bag with a round nozzle, then pipe it onto the edges of each cooled large macaron. Place the cherries in the centres and layer the filled macarons. Sandwich the small macarons in the same way.
10. Top the large macaron stack with the small macarons to decorate. Finish with a light dusting of icing sugar.

DARK CHOCOLATE CHEESECAKE

SERVES 8–10

350 g dark chocolate biscuits (I use Romany Creams)
50 g dark chocolate chips
100 g butter, melted
800 g plain cream cheese, room temperature
200 ml sour cream, room temperature
180 g castor sugar
40 g cocoa powder, sifted
1 Tbsp espresso granules
4 eggs
200 g dark chocolate, melted and cooled

FOR THE TOPPING

100 g dark chocolate, melted (optional)

1. Place the dark chocolate biscuits and dark chocolate chips into a food processor and pulse until fine. Mix in the melted butter, then press into a springform cake tin. Refrigerate while you make the filling.
2. Preheat the oven to 100 °C.
3. In a bowl, combine the cream cheese, sour cream, castor sugar, cocoa powder, espresso granules, eggs and melted dark chocolate, and mix until smooth. Pour the mixture onto the biscuit base.
4. Bake for about 1 hour 10 minutes, or until the cheesecake is set but the centre is still slightly wobbly. Remove from the oven and cool completely at room temperature. Then, refrigerate for at least 4 hours, or until completely set.
5. If preferred, drizzle the melted dark chocolate over the cold cheesecake, then slice and serve.

ORANGE SWISS ROLL

SERVES 8–10

FOR THE SPONGE

4 large eggs, room temperature
100 g castor sugar, plus 80 g, for dusting
1 tsp vanilla extract
90 g cake flour
2 tsp baking powder

FOR THE FILLING

1 cup whipping cream
2 Tbsp icing sugar
1 tsp vanilla extract
¼ cup orange marmalade
Extra whipped cream and orange slices, to decorate (optional)

1. Preheat the oven to 180 °C.
2. Line a rectangular baking tray (23 × 33 cm) with baking paper.
3. To make the sponge, use an electric beater to whisk the eggs, castor sugar and vanilla extract until the batter is thick and pale (this is called the ribbon stage).
4. In a separate bowl, sift together the flour and baking powder, then fold into the batter.
5. Pour the batter into the prepared baking tray and bake for 15–20 minutes, until the sponge is just set – it will spring back when touched. Do not overbake.
6. Dust castor sugar onto a clean tea towel. Flip the hot, baked sponge onto the tea towel. Peel away the baking-paper lining, then roll the sponge tightly in the tea towel (the towel should be wrapped within the roll of the sponge). Set aside to cool completely.
7. To make the filling, whisk the cream, icing sugar and vanilla exraxt to stiff peaks. Once the sponge has cooled completely, unwrap it from the tea towel. Spread the sponge with a layer of marmalade, followed by an even layer of whipped cream. Roll the sponge into a log to encase the filling and form the roll.
8. If preferred, decorate with extra whipped cream piped on top and slices of orange. Place the Swiss roll in the fridge for 30 minutes to firm before slicing and serving.

CINNAMON ROLLS

MAKES 12

FOR THE DOUGH

2 eggs
1 cup milk
100 g butter, melted
4 cups cake flour
10 g instant dry yeast
2 tsp ground cinnamon
1 tsp ground nutmeg
¼ tsp ground allspice
1 cup raisins
1 cup white sugar
Zest of 1 naartjie/clementine
1 tsp vegetable oil

FOR THE FILLING

100 g butter, softened
1 cup dark brown sugar
3 tsp ground cinnamon
1 tsp vanilla extract

FOR THE TOPPING

125 g plain cream cheese, room temperature
50 g butter, softened
1 tsp vanilla extract
½ cup castor sugar
Juice of ½ naartjie/clementine (use the same one that you used for the zest)

1. To make the dough, start by whisking together the eggs, milk and melted butter in a bowl.
2. In a separate bowl, mix the flour, yeast, cinnamon, nutmeg, allspice, raisins, white sugar and naartjie zest.
3. Gradually add the wet ingredients to the dry ingredients, while mixing, until a dough forms. Use as much or as little of the wet-ingredient mixture as you need, and add water if your dough is too dry. Knead the dough for 5–8 minutes, until it is smooth and elastic.
4. Drizzle the vegetable oil into a bowl. Roll the dough in the oil, then leave it in the bowl. Cover with a damp cloth or cling wrap and leave to rise until it has doubled in size, then knead it back to its original size. Roll it out into a rectangle (about 5 mm thick).
5. To make the filling, mix the softened butter, dark brown sugar, cinnamon and vanilla extract until smooth. Spread the mixture evenly over the dough.
6. Roll the dough into a log, from one long edge to the other. Pinch the seam to close.
7. Cut the log into 12 slices, then place them onto a lined baking tray, cut-side up. Cover with a damp cloth or cling wrap and leave to rise for 30 minutes.
8. In the meantime, preheat the oven to 180 °C.
9. Bake the rolls for 30–40 minutes, until they have risen and turned golden brown. Optional: glaze the buns by brushing them with a tablespoon of marmalade as they come out of the oven, then set aside to cool for 10 minutes.
10. To make the topping, mix the cream cheese, butter, vanilla extract, castor sugar and naartjie juice. Spread the topping generously over the warm buns.

LEMON MERINGUE PIE

FOR THE CRUST

200 g coconut biscuits, crushed

100 g butter, melted

FOR THE FILLING

3 large egg yolks

1 can (385 g) sweetened condensed milk

½ cup lemon juice

FOR THE TOPPING

3 large egg whites

¾ cup castor sugar

1 tsp vanilla extract

1. Preheat the oven to 180 °C.
2. Mix together the crushed coconut biscuits and melted butter, then press the mixture into a 20 cm fluted, loose-bottom tart tin. Make sure you press the mixture up the sides of the tin as well as on the bottom. Place into the fridge to firm while you make the filling.
3. To make the filling, mix the egg yolks, condensed milk and lemon juice in a bowl. Strain the mixture into the chilled crust.
4. Bake the pie for 30 minutes, until the mixture is set with a slight jiggle in the centre. Remove from the oven and allow to cool completely.
5. To make the topping, in a large heatproof bowl, combine the egg whites and castor sugar. Place the mixture over a pot of simmering water (the water should not touch the bowl) and stir until the sugar dissolves. Remove from the heat, add the vanilla extract and whisk with an electric beater until the mixture is cool and the egg whites have become light, fluffy and glossy. Spoon over the chilled pie. Store the pie in the fridge if not serving straight away.

OPTIONAL

You can toast the top of the pie using a blowtorch, or by placing it under the grill in the oven for a few minutes until golden.

BAKED NUTTY APPLE PUDDING

SERVES 6–8

4 apples, peeled and diced
75 g brown sugar
40 g butter
1 cup chopped pecans

FOR THE PUDDING
175 ml water
225 g pitted dates, chopped
1 tsp bicarbonate of soda
85 g butter, plus more for greasing
140 g brown sugar
1 tsp vanilla essence
2 eggs
2 Tbsp molasses
175 g self-raising flour
100 ml milk

FOR THE SAUCE
175 g brown sugar
50 g butter
1 cup cream
1 Tbsp golden syrup

1. Add the apples, sugar, and butter to a pan. Cook over medium heat until the apples begin to caramelise, then stir in the pecans. Remove from the heat and set aside.
2. To make the pudding, add the water to a saucepan and bring to a boil. Add the dates and boil for 5 minutes to soften, then stir in the bicarbonate of soda. Remove from the heat and set aside to cool.
3. Grease a 2-litre oven dish, then preheat the oven to 180 °C.
4. Cream the butter, brown sugar and vanilla essence until light and fluffy. Mix in the eggs, one at a time, until well combined. Add the molasses, then fold in the flour and milk.
5. Stir in the softened dates and caramelised apples, then transfer the mixture to the prepared oven dish. Bake for about 40–45 minutes, until the pudding has risen and is firm to the touch. Once baked, remove the pudding from the oven.
6. To make the sauce, add all the sauce ingredients to a pot and heat gently over low heat until melted, stirring continuously. Bring to a boil and simmer for about 5 minutes, or until thickened. Pour the sauce over the pudding.

ROOIBOS APPLE CRUMBLE

SERVES 6

FOR THE APPLES

10 apples, peeled and chopped
¼ cup white sugar
1 tsp ground cinnamon
½ cup brewed rooibos tea

FOR THE CRUMBLE

1 cup cake flour
1 tsp baking powder
100 g cold butter, diced
1 cup white sugar
½ cup oats
½ cup desiccated coconut
Leaves from 2 rooibos teabags, ground into a fine powder

1. Preheat the oven to 180 °C.
2. To make the apples, combine the apples, sugar, cinnamon and rooibos tea in a pot, and cook until the apples begin to soften. Transfer to a baking dish.
3. To make the crumble, sift together the flour and baking powder, then rub in the butter until the mixture resembles breadcrumbs. Mix in the sugar, oats, coconut and rooibos tea leaves. The mixture should resemble a crumbly dough.
4. Sprinkle the crumble over the apples, then bake for 30–40 minutes, until golden and crisp.

ROOIBOS APPLE CRUMBLE

RECIPE INDEX

Published in 2022 by Penguin Books, an imprint of
Penguin Random House South Africa (Pty) Ltd
Company Reg. No. 1953/000441/07

The Estuaries, 4 Oxbow Crescent, Century Avenue,
Century City 7441, Cape Town, South Africa
PO Box 1144, Cape Town, 8000, South Africa

www.penguinrandomhouse.co.za

PUBLISHER: Beverley Dodd
MANAGING EDITOR AND EDITOR: Aimee Carelse
DESIGNER: Randall Watson
PROOFREADER AND INDEXER : Gill Gordon
PHOTOGRAPHER AND PROP STYLIST: Matanna Katz
FOOD STYLIST: Zola Nene
FOOD STYLIST'S ASSISTANTS:
Sebastian Newman, Lana Samuels

Special thanks to
Vorster & Braye Ceramic Design
for the ceramic props

REPRODUCTION: Studio Repro
Printed and bound in Parow,
Cape Town by Shumani RSA

ISBN: 978-1-48590-126-6